John Keats *and the Sonnet Tradition:*

A CRITICAL AND COMPARATIVE STUDY

John Keats *and the Sonnet Tradition:*

A CRITICAL AND COMPARATIVE STUDY

BY

LAWRENCE JOHN ZILLMAN

1966

OCTAGON BOOKS, INC.

New York

For Lorene: *This, our book*

PREFACE

Despite the evidence from Keats himself—numbers, commentary on, and experiments with the form—that the poet was keenly interested in the sonnet, scholars and critics have, in the past, given relatively little attention to this part of his work. Such attention as the quatorzains have received has been mainly with regard to chronology, biographical allusions, and structural relationship to the odes. With the appearance of Claude Lee Finney's remarkably complete study of the evolution of Keats's poetry the matter of chronology and relationship to reading and environmental influences has been made nearly certain, for the sonnets as for the general poems. But Mr. Finney himself is forced to say at one point in his study: "In adopting the Petrarchan form of the sonnet Keats followed the fashion of the period. I cannot show, however, that he took the sonnets of a particular poet, such as Milton, Wordsworth, or Hunt, as his definite models."

The failure to show such models lies not in lack of thoroughness but in method of approach. Mr. Finney has, as have most others, placed a minimum of emphasis on versecraft, a maximum on phrase parallels, reading backgrounds, etc. Clearly the poem and the poet's style are ultimately the blend of all these elements, and the present work attempts to throw some light on the neglected phase of the problem: the versecraft of Keats's sonnets in respect to the historical development of the form and its use by representative English sonneteers. For the technical influence of writer on writer, or the place of the poet in the historical development of a form, will frequently be shown more completely and more clearly by a comparison of this type than is possible by a study of parallels in words, ideas, and phrases which may be quite general to an age.

At the same time it has seemed desirable to offer, in the first part of the study, a re-evaluation of the sonnet as a literary form. The writings of a group of purists in the past few years have tended to emphasize the concept of what they feel a sonnet should be, rather than of what it actually has been in its historical vicissitudes. Possibly the true goal of sonnet legislation lies somewhere between: it will not be amiss to view both sides as a basis for judgment.

I am sincerely grateful for the kindness, in days already full, of Dean F. M. Padelford, Professors D. D. Griffith and E. G. Cox of the University of Washington, and J. Randolph Sasnett, who read the manuscript and offered valuable suggestions.

LAWRENCE J. ZILLMAN

University of Washington
October 1, 1939

TABLE OF CONTENTS

John Keats *and the Sonnet Tradition:*

A CRITICAL AND COMPARATIVE STUDY

Part One:

The Sonnet and Its Status in the Age of Keats

The genius of poetry must work out its own salvation in a man: it cannot be matured by law and precept, but by sensation and watch-fulness in itself. That which is creative must create itself.

[Letter to James Hessey,
October 9, 1818.]

ON THE SONNET

If by dull rhymes our English must be chain'd,
And, like Andromeda, the Sonnet sweet
Fetter'd, in spite of pained loveliness,
Let us find out, if we must be constrain'd,
Sandals more interwoven and complete
To fit the naked foot of Poesy:
Let us inspect the Lyre, and weigh the stress
Of every chord, and see what may be gain'd
By ear industrious, and attention meet;
Misers of sound and syllable, no less
Than Midas of his coinage, let us be
Jealous of dead leaves in the bay wreath crown;
So, if we may not let the Muse be free,
She will be bound with garlands of her own.

[April, 1819]

THE SONNET AND ITS STATUS
IN THE AGE OF KEATS

Two periods in English literature stand out above others as particularly fertile in the use of new poetic forms. The first, centering around the reign of Elizabeth, was in many respects the blossoming time of English prosody, an age of experiment that brought into its literature new moods, new techniques, and a freedom, never since equaled, in adapting exotic structures to a growing language. But, following the first half of the seventeenth century which culminated in Milton, a retreat into formalism overshadowed much of this accomplishment, and a coldness of restraint limited most of the poetry for a hundred years to the stiffness of the closed heroic couplet.

A period so mechanical in its effects as was the age of Anne could not, of course, narrow the creative channel for long, and as the stream of literature followed the turn into the nineteenth century it once more found the broader sweep that marks the creative as opposed to the critical attitude. The rigidity of Pope's couplets gave way in "Endymion" to a freedom surpassing even that of Chaucer; blank verse fulfilled the promise made for it by Milton and became the most vital meter for longer poems; the Spenserian stanza lost the archaisms that marked it as imitative in the eighteenth century, and found a new and modern richness in the last cantos of "Childe Harold," in "The Eve of St. Agnes," and in "Adonais"; and the sonnet, after a hesitant and technically crude renaissance among the poetasters of the late eighteenth century, finally won a victory for lyrical verse commensurate with that of the other forms for narrative and descriptive verse. It found a justification—particularly in the works of

Wordsworth, Hunt, and Keats—both in creative expression and theoretical clarification that assured it the important place it still holds.

Since the early nineteenth century we have come far in the definition and legislation of our poetic patterns—so far, indeed, that there is some tendency to lose sight of a basis for proper critical judgment. This is particularly true of the sonnet. It is necessary, for example, to disabuse oneself immediately of the notion that there was in Keats's lifetime a well-defined and authoritative canon which compares in any measure with the legislation more recently formulated. That these later attempts have been entirely successful is still open to question; such Procrustean demands as some modern theorists would assign to the quatorzain may be helpful in setting pedagogic goals at which young verse writers can shoot, but they fail to recognize the historical vicissitudes through which the form has passed, or the modifications through which it must continue to pass so long as the creative mind is different from the critical.

In fairness to the poet, then, we must approach the examination of Keats's sonnets not through a narrow dogma, but through his own background. Such an approach does not deny us the use of modern terminology or analytical method; it merely limits us to an assumption of intent on Keats's part commensurate with the backgrounds of theory and practice available to him. And in the light of that background and theory it will be well first to describe briefly the patterns and modifications known to the poet, and to indicate the meager critical opinion that might have influenced his attitude towards the quatorzain.

Of the patterns, three—the Italian, Shakespearean, and Spenserian—were established by Keats's day. These were the sonnet forms that had proved best

suited to the needs of the English language, and that
had stood the test of from two to three centuries' time
in winning out above numerous rather widely diver-
gent quatorzain novelties.* Of these three patterns
the poet used only the first two in his own work, but
the bearing of the third on the development of the
others (and the reasonable certainty that Keats knew
the sonnets of Spenser) leads us to admit it to the
following characterization.

2

Historically, sonnet beginnings centered about the
Italian, or Petrarchan, pattern. The origins—variously ascribed to the Sicilian backgrounds of Piero,
to classical ode and epigram, or to a lyrical ancestry
in Provence—are still uncertain, but it is possible to
see, beginning about the thirteenth century, a line of
development—leading through Piero delle Vigne [or
Pietro della Vigne] (1190-1249), Fra Guittone
d'Arezzo (c. 1230-94), and Dante—that finally culminated in Petrarch, the large output and prestige of
whose work quickly made it the norm.

The use made of the Italian pattern by Petrarch and
others since his day offers convincing proof that the
structure is admirably suited to the expression of emotion in lyrical mood. The fourteen co-ordinated

---

*Among such deviations used by recognized writers the following are typical:
1. Caudated or tailed: with "tails" of from two to six verses.
2. Duodenary or versi sdruccioli: twelve-syllabled lines ending in dactyls.
3. Mute: all rimes of the one syllable type.
4. Continuous or iterating: on one rime throughout, or on two rimes.
5. Answering: in answer to other sonnets, with rimes repeated in exact correspondence, but with dissimilar meanings.
6. Retrograde: reading the same backwards as forwards.
7. Chained or linked: each verse beginning with the last word of the preceding verse; also applied to those of the Spenserian type.
8. Interwoven: with medial as well as end rime.
9. Crowning: a series joined together for panegyric, to form a supposed crown.

[Based on Hunt's "Essay" and Sharp's "The Sonnet."]

NOTE: Only those notes carrying supplementary information will be included *passim*. These will be indicated by asterisks. Identification or source
notes, numbered, will be found beginning p. 199.

verses offer a medium that is at once long enough to serve for the reasonably complete treatment of a single or a limited number of ideas or emotions, and to provide ample verses for emphasis on sectional structure —and at the same time it is brief enough to require careful discipline on the part of the writer, that his idea may be artistically expressed without suffering from overcompression; and brief enough also to enable the reader to grasp easily the balance between parts coupled with the unity of the whole.

Whether because the average reader is limited in his ability to retain, as a single impression, extended passages of lyrical material, or because songs and brief themes naturally tend to fall into two parts, complementary or antithetical, the Italian sonnet since the earliest times has had a characteristic division into two sections. Further, since the second part is in a measure the outgrowth of the first, and develops with a knowledge of the first assumed, it is properly the briefer of the two, the sections being of eight (the octave) and six (the sestet) verses respectively. This distribution gives ample opportunity for restrained development of theme, while the difference in rime scheme between the two parts emphasizes their normally complementary nature. Smaller units (quatrains and tercets) are possible in the natural divisions of octave and sestet, but their emphasis will depend largely on organization of subject matter by the poet.

The basic iambic pentameter verse offers the element of dignity demanded by the usual sonnet themes. It is restrained, and less likely to break into metronomic movement than would be the tetrameter or hexameter.

The above elements, leading to a desirable variety within the larger unity of the whole, are further fused by the rime scheme. This, in the Italian sonnet, em-

phasizes the two-part division, the octave usually
employing the pattern *abbaabba* and the sestet being
about equally divided between *cdcdcd* and *cdecde*.
The octave is thus framed in an admirably unified pattern from which relatively little deviation has been
made, while the sestet permits much greater freedom,
and gives the poet an opportunity for individuality in
formulating a close that will be "simple, conclusive,
and satisfactory."[1]

The effect of the *abbaabba* octave is truly remarkable. It is actually a blend of three brace-rime quatrains, since the middle four verses, whose sounds over-
lap the others and echo their pattern, impress the
reader with a similar sound relationship, thus,
ab*baab*ba. Normally, too, a definite pause is made in
the thought development at the end of the eighth
verse, serving to increase the independent unity of an
octave that has already progressed with the greatest
economy in rime sounds. In the distribution of these
sounds, also, the reader retains the opening verse ending until its final satisfaction in the eighth verse, while
at the same time he receives, progressively, echoes of
both the *a* and *b* sounds. Certainly it would be difficult to conceive a more artistically compact and pho-
nologically more effective pattern, and it is scarcely
surprising that so many English poets (with the remarkable exceptions of Spenser and Shakespeare) have
found in the Italian form the medium for lyrics of
exquisite beauty.

But while consistent use of patterns other than
abbaabba has been slight, it should not be thought that
this octave reached the nineteenth century without
attempts at modification by those who have made the
sonnet what it is. There have been two basic variations that have received fairly wide use, the first of
which employs alternation instead of the conventional

brace rime, and the second of which introduces a new sound in the sixth and seventh verses, giving the scheme *abbaacca*. The latter use did not gain wide acceptance in Italy, but it found favor in Spain as early as the fourteenth century, and it is the octave pattern for almost half of the sonnets of Wordsworth. It is obviously less unified than the normal pattern and, while it has the advantage of making some concessions to a language as poor in rime words as is English, it may offend the sensitive ear, like "some new strain in a melody that is already in itself amply sufficient, and that loses in effect by the alien introduction."[2]

Michelangelo, Milton, and Keats are among those who have held invariably to the normal *abbaabba* of the Italian octave, while among those[3] who have employed variations are Petrarch (14 occurrences of alternation in 317 sonnets), Dante (7 alternating type in 43 sonnets), Leigh Hunt (1 alternating type in the 28 written before 1819, which might therefore have influenced Keats), and Wordsworth, the great variety of whose octaves in more than 500 Italian sonnets may be observed in Table I.[4]

TABLE I

WORDSWORTH'S OCTAVE PATTERNS

Pattern	Occurrences	Pattern	Occurrences
abbaabba	224	abbabaab	4
abbaacca	205	ababcaca	3
abababba	12	abbabccb	2
ababbaab	12	ababbabab	2
ababbccb	11	ababbaba	2
abbaabab	10	ababcbcb	2
abbababa	8	ababacac	1
abbacaca	8	abbacaac	1
abbaacac	7	ababbcbc	1
ababacca	5		

The sestet of the Italian sonnet has been the subject of much controversy in the adaptation of the form to its English use. This is owing in large part to the greater freedom in rime scheme that has always been allowed to this division of the sonnet (see Table II[5]), and to the early tendency on the part of English writers to lead into a concluding couplet. The arguments regarding the latter, especially, have ranged between the extremes of dogmatic exclusion and moderate defense. The purists will say that "no sestet should contain a rhymed couplet or couplets and a sestet may not end with a rhymed couplet. . . . The final rhymed couplet belongs exclusively to the Shakespearean sonnet and must not be used in a modern

TABLE II*
COMPARATIVE SESTET PATTERNS

Pattern	Occurrences						
	M'angelo	Dante	Petrarch	Milton	Wordsworth	Hunt	Keats
cdecde	56	5	122	5	34	11	6
cdcdcd	6	9	115	7	63	6	24
cdedce	0	11	64	2	31	1	1
cdccdc	1	5	9	0	0	0	0
cdddcc	0	5	4	0	0	0	0
cdeedc	0	8	1	0	9	0	0
cdedec	0	0	1	0	17	0	4
cdcdee	0	0	0	0	38	3	3
cddcdc	0	0	0	1	49	0	2
cdcddc	0	0	0	0	42	0	1
cdcede	0	0	0	0	20	0	1
cddcee	0	0	0	1	62	2	2
cdceed	0	0	0	1	19	0	0
cdccdd	0	0	0	0	0	0	1

English sonnet in any circumstances."[6] Others make certain concessions to such a close. Of these Thomas Hutchinson is typical when he writes, "The objection against a closing couplet lies only when the rhyme-sound is *new; i. e.* has not been heard earlier in the sonnet: as in the forms, *abbacc* [*i. e. cddcee*] and *ababcc* [*cdcdee*],"[7] and he lists *cdddcc* as satisfactory.

To the purists it might be suggested that if the closing couplet is appropriate to one form of the sonnet (as such) it should be appropriate to all; and it might be observed further that since the octave has actually progressed through what are in effect three

*As might be supposed, Wordsworth uses extreme variety in sestet patterns, and his second and fifth preferences (by occurrences) close on independent couplet rimes. Other patterns used by Wordsworth include: *cdeced* (29); *cddccd* (27) ; *cddece* (18) ; *cdeecd* (15) ; *ccdeed* (13) ; *ccdede* (12). Figures for Hunt are for the 28 sonnets (exclusive of the *Juvenilia*) written before 1819, which therefore might have influenced Keats. Other patterns used by Hunt are: *ccdcdd* (4) ; *cdecfe* (1). The *cdcdcd* figure for Keats includes one sestet, *cdcd[]d*, with an unrimed shortened thirteenth verse.

couplets *(abbaabba)*, the closing couplet may therefore logically be a desirable repetition of a basic device,
and serve to unify by recurrence.*

The flaw in all such arguments (including the
latter) is that attention is focused entirely on the rime
scheme, and fails to take into account the poet's development of thought and phrasing, which may be so
controlled as practically to discount the importance of
rime pattern. It can never completely do so, since
there must always be a sound echo in the reader's mind,
but these echoes can unquestionably be made subordi-
nate to thought development. The poetic basis for
justification or condemnation of the closing couplet
should, therefore, be more catholic in its scope. If
the poet is dealing with the sonnet as a medium for
the completely unified expression of a single or of
closely related ideas, and is striving for singleness of
impression, he obviously should not prejudice his
chances for this unity by permitting the last two verses
of his sonnet to stand out from the others in a sharply
turned couplet. To be sure, he must of necessity risk
the loss of *complete* unity by the octave-sestet division,
which is, even in the Miltonic use (characterized below), an inherent part of the structure. The division
may, however, logically result in a balance that need
not deny unity, since a complement of six verses
against eight has obviously more chance of artistic
success than has that of two against twelve.

But the close described by Hunt as "simple, conclusive, and satisfactory" may sometimes, he adds, be
"epigrammatic ... where the subject warrants it, or
where point of that kind is desirable."[8] It is not diffi-

---

*Denial of the couplet to the Italian sonnet cannot be made on historical
grounds. Smart suggests [*The Sonnets of Milton*, p. 17] that Wyatt's preference
for the couplet may have been the result of his following Fazio degli Uberti,
who influenced Tasso; and shows [p. 19] that Antonio Minturno, in *L'Arte
Poetica*, favored a wide variety of quatrains and tercets because variety is
pleasant in lyrical poetry.

cult to imagine a sonnet organization in which the first
twelve verses of the Italian form, from the nature of
the thought content, would find an effective and even
a striking turn through the addition of a closing couplet. In other words, the rime pattern should not determine, but support, a corresponding thought pattern; and many of our English Petrarchan sonnets
(e. g. numbers 2 and 23 by Keats) do actually close
with the thought in couplet form, summarizing or
complementing what has gone before, even without
benefit of rime correspondence.

In general, however, the Spenserian and Shakespearean modifications of the Italian sonnet offer better progression towards the closing couplet, and if the
objectionable "must" can be avoided, we would agree
that closing the Petrarchan form with this device is
normally not conducive to the attainment of the
highest artistic unity. Furthermore, since the sestet
usually serves as a balancing variant to the octave, and
since the octave contains what are in effect three
modified couplets, a more artistic variation will be
gained by avoiding any couplets in the sestet. The two
most widely used patterns, *cdecde* and *cdcdcd*, suggest that the finest poetic minds favor this conclusion,
though Wordsworth stands as a remarkable exception
to the statement.

The possibility of further division in the octave
and sestet units should be noted. The *abbaabba* pattern
obviously suggests two closely interlinked quatrains,
and it is not uncommon to find the thought developing to a pause at the end of verse four—reaching a
minor climax at that point—and then, following a
slight shift in attack, leading to a major climax at the
end of verse eight, this in turn being followed by a
balancing conclusion in the sestet. The sestet, too,
especially in the *cdecde* pattern, is likewise suscep-

tible of division, into two tercets. But there is ample
precedent for ignoring such pauses when the subject
warrants it, and again the basis of judgment should
be the artistic relationship between form and content.

The reasonable conclusion suggested by even such
a cursory examination of the technical aspect of sonnet structure as the foregoing is that a form at once so
admirably unified and interestingly varied can and
should never be legislated into rigidity so long as
there are poets to write and sonnets to be written. The
discipline requisite to all art must, of course, be
stressed, but no form should be so dogmatically determined that it ceases to be susceptible of infusion
with poetic imagination.* This is true also of sonnet
subject matter, and it should be observed that, popular
opinion to the contrary, the Italians themselves by no
means confined the sonnet to the subject of love,
though amatory themes dominated the sequences. A
wide range of subjects, including general compliment,
friendship, hostility, and poetic epistle may be found
in the earliest extant quatorzains, and since the sixteenth century almost no limits have been set on sonnet
themes.

3

Before considering the Miltonic use of and contribution to the Italian sonnet it will be well, in the interest of historical perspective, to note briefly the conditions under which the pattern was introduced into

---

*Let us not forget Keats's description of the versifiers of the age of Anne:
                    . . . with a puling infant's force
          They sway'd about upon a rocking horse,
          And thought it Pegasus . . .
                              were closely wed
          To musty laws lined out with wretched rule
          And compass vile: so that ye taught a school
          Of dolts to smooth, inlay, and clip, and fit,
          Till, like the certain wands of Jacob's wit,
          Their verses tallied.
                    ["Sleep and Poetry," ll. 185-87, 194-99]

England, and the early modifications from which it was necessary for Milton to appeal directly to Italian sources that the original structure might become a part of English prosody. For the modifications gave rise to the Spenserian and Shakespearean patterns, basic to Elizabethan England though in a sense offshoots of the Petrarchan form; and with the Shakespearean particularly, Keats was to become significantly associated in a relationship similar to that of Milton for the Italian.

Under the impetus of the Renaissance early sixteenth-century England experienced a revival of interest in the writers and literature of Italy that was to result in vital innovations for Elizabethan and later poetry. A century and a half earlier Chaucer had enriched the limited stock of English stanzas by his use of the heroic couplet, the rime royal, and other patterns well adapted to the needs of a growing language. But it was left for Sir Thomas Wyatt and Henry Howard, Earl of Surrey, to introduce the two poetic forms that have been, above all others, the most widely used from their day to our own—blank verse and the sonnet.

To Surrey is reserved a double literary importance. By translating two books of Vergil's "Aeneid" into blank verse he used for the first time in England the unrimed heroic meter that was to dominate the drama for a century, to be taken into the field of nondramatic poetry by Milton, and, after a brief eclipse by the Popean couplet, to become established as the most flexible and individually adaptable English form. And by carrying on the experiments begun by Wyatt, Surrey was to arrive at greater technical perfection in adapting the pentameter line to sonnet use, and was to hit upon that rime scheme best suited to a language poor in rime sounds, but which was to take its name from one who used the form with greater distinction than he—the Shakespearean or English pattern.

To Wyatt, however, the more prolific of these two early sonneteers, must be accorded the credit for introducing the form and taking the first steps in adapting it to English use. Primarily concerned with the subject matter of courtly and refined love which he found in the Italian sonnets, Wyatt seems to have been satisfied with an approximation to the Petrarchan structure. Thus, while imitating and even translating the content of Petrarch, the form was permitted to adjust itself as best it could (and frequently with extreme clumsiness) to the demands and difficulties of a language so different from the original as is English. These adjustments are most pronounced in the rime schemes; for while Wyatt conforms fairly closely to the octave pattern of Petrarch, he habitually adds a sestet on the pattern *cddcee*. Although this pattern is not found in Petrarch's work it undoubtedly occurred in the sonnets of some less famous writer known to Wyatt—possibly, as Smart suggests, in those of Fazio degli Uberti.[9] Regardless of its source, the couplet was to become established as the mode for closing the English sonnet in the period of Elizabeth, thus vindicating Wyatt's judgment, and was to enjoy some vogue even after Milton's appeal to authority a century later had reasserted the normal Italian technique.

Wyatt obviously should not be criticized for departing from the so-called "regular" Petrarchan form, since he had ample precedent for most of the arrangements that occur in his work. It is only through the perspective of the centuries that we are able to determine the nature and distinctive qualities of the "regular" pattern, and to see its predominance

in the great body of sonnets dating from fifteenth-
century Italy. Wyatt could know only the relatively
few poems he had seen, and there was evidence even
in those of Petrarch (to say nothing of his contemporaries) that the only restrictions were number and
length of verses, and general division of thought between octave and sestet.

4

Following the experiments of Wyatt and Surrey,
other writers of the Elizabethan period made extensive
use of the sonnet.* Sidney, influenced mainly by
Wyatt, made it the unit of the first sequence in English, "Astrophel and Stella," and he was followed by
many others, among them Watson, Daniel, Lodge,
Barnes, Giles Fletcher, Constable, Drayton, Spenser,
and Shakespeare, whose cycles lent praise to their real
or ideal loves.

Many of these sonnets illustrate the wide variety of
patterns through which the form was passing in its
adaptation to the demands of English, especially in the
matter of rime schemes. The abundance of rime
sounds in Italian contrasted sharply with their paucity ˋ
in English, and the result, naturally, was that the complicated and sharply emphasized pattern of the conventional Petrarchan octave offered serious difficulties
to writers who, for the most part as experimenters,
were attempting to work in the newly introduced
medium. Other structural problems, while recognized,
took second place to the question of rime distribution.
And out of the period of experimentation there

---

*But the lack of critical attention to the sonnet at this time will be sug-
gested by the fact that in the two lengthy volumes of Gregory Smith's *Elizabethan Critical Essays* only three writers even mention the form: George
Gascoigne, who refers to it as a six- or ten-line stanza used by the French;
King James VI, who describes it as fourteen lines with ten feet in each line;
and Sir John Harrington, who is primarily interested in sonnet "scurrilitie."

emerged two basically English forms, the Spenserian
and the Shakespearean, to stand beside the Italian.

The form used by Spenser in his "Amoretti" (with
one Shakespearean exception) offers what is, in effect,
a transitional pattern. Its rime scheme, *abab bcbc
cdcd ee,* avoids the sound emphasis found in the braced
Italian octave, yet possesses something of the com-
pactness of that form in the interlinking of the
quatrains. It is quite probable that the pattern was
particularly congenial to this poet because of its
close relationship to the Spenserian stanza, the first
eight verses of which parallel the opening two sonnet
quatrains. In the stanza scheme, *ababbcbcc* (the ninth
verse of which is an Alexandrine), the same interlinking effect will be observed. The transitional nature of the Spenserian sonnet is thus to be found in the
distribution of a relatively small number of rime words
to obtain a more "open" development than is possible
with the brace-rime octave.

Instead of a closely knit two-part division between
octave and sestet, the sonnet is seen now to be developing through three quatrains and a closing couplet, the latter not infrequently being epigrammatic or
sharply turned. The couplet, as noted above, tends to
deny the nature of the Petrarchan form, the beauty of
which lies largely in its total unity of impression and
in the retention by the reader of sounds that build into
the very heart of the sonnet. Yet, while the greater
freedom would seem desirable for the needs of English,
the sonnet of Spenser has never gained a wide following. This is the result, in part, of the still greater freedom of the Shakespearean form, and of the supremacy
of Shakespeare's genius, but it must also be recognized
that the Spenserian sonnet as a pattern does not have
the organic unity and effectiveness of the Spenserian
stanza, and seems a rather weak compromise. Whether

or not Keats realized these shortcomings, he has left, as has been said, no example of the form, and this despite his great admiration for, and his constant study of, Spenser. He was probably influenced quite as much by Leigh Hunt's dislike for the pattern as by his own independent observations. Hunt is very definite in his condemnation:

> The rhyme seems at once less responsive and always interfering; and the music has no longer its major and minor divisions. It is not indeed easy to conceive what induced the inventor of the beautiful stanza of the "Fairie Queene," with its fine organ-like close, to employ so inferior a construction in all these eighty-eight sonnets called the *Amoretti*. Finding perhaps how much his first rhyming invention was admired, he too hastily thought to succeed in another, and failed as authors' second enterprizes, when so suggested, are apt to fail.... Yet Spenser, in his mature days, never wrote but one sonnet in any other form. To my ear there is something in it of the teasing nature of Dante's *terza rima*, which is a chain that seems as if it would never end, and is dragged after him by the presumptuous poet through his next world, like a retribution.[10]

For whatever reason, it has been true that if the Italian form does not meet a poet's need he will usually turn to the fairly free and admirably suited English or Shakespearean form. In this pattern, which became widely popular in Shakespeare's day and has continued second only to the Petrarchan, the rime alternation and the three-quatrain-plus-couplet organization of Spenser are carried to their logical freedom by removing the interlinking rimes.* The principal novelty of the resulting *abab cdcd efef gg* pattern is to be found in the completely new set of rimes in each of the quatrains. This arrangement, unknown in Italy, was only hinted at in Spenser's use and in the early sixteenth-

*Ridley [*Keats' Craftsmanship*, p. 198] says that Milton chose the Italian form because of its greater freedom. Surely such a statement cannot be based on an understanding of the technical demands of the patterns.

century experiments, and (although considered "unartistical" by Leigh Hunt) it brought the form into
its most compatible relationship with the scarcity of
English rime sounds. On the other hand, however, it
destroys even more completely than does the Spenserian form the octave-sestet balance and unity of the
Italian sonnet. In the Shakespearean pattern there is
nothing of the unifying technique inherent in the
Italian form, and each quatrain stands, as regards
pattern, independent of the others. This independence
is increased by the use of alternating rime, which
leads forward to the end of each quatrain more progressively and more swiftly than can either brace-rime
or interlinking quatrains; and, being unlinked as is
the Spenserian form, the independent alternating pattern tends to set off the quatrains in which it is used.
The thought, of course, may still be made to conform
to a two-part division; but just as octave balanced by
sestet invites a corresponding development of thought,
so three independent quatrains to which a couplet is
added suggest a correspondence in thought progression suitable to the changed pattern. Even a cursory
examination of the sonnets of Spenser and Shakespeare
will show that this is borne out in practice, as both
two-part sonnets and those emphasizing three parts
plus couplet are abundant.*

Thus by the turn of the century the Elizabethans
had enriched their prosody with the sonnet forms; and

---

*It is on this point particularly that the theory of T. W. H. Crosland [*The
English Sonnet*] breaks down. Having contended that *all* sonnets must be of the
two-part type, he selects only those that illustrate his point, and deliberately
avoids evidence that would disprove his contention, or refuses to admit examples of it as sonnets. His definition and legislation are thus not based on the
existing sonnet, but are attempts to limit examples of the form by laws unknown
to the writers.

Crosland's further contention that heroic verse in general has the sonnet for
its ancestor, that blank verse resulted from omission of rimes in the sonnet,
and that many blank-verse or heroic-couplet passages are sonnets except in
rime scheme, is original but scarcely tenable. Where defendable, he is merely
saying that great passages of poetry may be found both in and out of sonnets,
and that lyrical passages cannot be sustained for many lines, a statement
Edgar Allan Poe anticipated by many years.

if the English adaptations seemed better suited to their needs than did the original Petrarchan, and so assumed a place of superiority, it was not to be for long—only until the prestige of Milton could be balanced against that of Shakespeare and bring the Italian form once more into a position of repute. The style and themes of the Elizabethans were also to undergo changes, as we shall see. But one should not condemn these early writers for the ornate style and the frequently repeated themes; one should realize, rather, that the conceits, the repetition of stock phrases and ideas, and even the exuberant richness, were all a part of the Italian heritage, as they were a part of the Elizabethan period itself; should realize, too, that a wide range of experimentation both in form and theme preceded Milton, in Italy as well as in England, and that Milton's "position among the writers of the sonnet is not due to any sudden breaking away from an outworn convention. It is due to his greatness as a poet, the wide compass of his powers, the extent of his reading, his many-sided character, and his interest in life, literature, society, politics and religion. He was free from the two marked failings of earlier English sonneteers —indiscriminate borrowing and self-repetition."[11]

5

If others anticipated the innovations of Milton, it was, nevertheless, to him and not to them that later writers were to turn for their model; and it was a model widely different in subject matter and form from those of his English predecessors. Milton was obviously turning, as he so frequently did, not to the earlier literary periods of his own country, but to the original wells from which his countrymen had dipped; and the waters were transmuted in passing into his own work. The result was a sonnet different from those of either Shakespeare or Petrarch, though closer in form to the latter.

In the obvious matter of rime schemes Milton, with one exception, is rigid enough to please the most fastidious. The exception, occurring only once in the entire body of eighteen quatorzains in English, is the inclusion in the sestet of a brace-rime quatrain followed by a closing couplet on a new rime sound, *cddcee*. The other sestet patterns, as noted in Table II, conform to the more normal Italian practice, and all the octaves are of the regular *abbaabba* type. His is, then, basically the Italian model so far as vertical pattern is concerned. But when a comparison is made with other sonnet characteristics it is evident at once that the poet is departing from tradition.

In the first place, only one sonnet by Milton has love for its theme; and this despite the cycles of the Elizabethans, the "Vita Nuova," and Petrarch's sonnets to Laura. Not but that he could find precedent for the themes of friendship, attack, appeal, defense, and those personal subjects which make up his total, but we have seen that in his predecessors such themes were the exception rather than the rule—that the dominant tone of the bulk of all sonnets before Milton had been amatory. More than this, the sequential nature of love sonnets had frequently resulted in little more than poetic exercises. That Milton wrote only eighteen sonnets, and these on nonrelated themes, would indicate that each was separately and sincerely inspired, a fact that would add to their importance and popularity in a field where readers may well have become sated with ventures into the "sugared" cycles.

In the second place, the difference in texture between the sonnets of Milton and those of his forerunners, which is only in part the result of his char-

acteristic latinisms and inversions, is immediately
sensed when they are read. R. D. Havens has described the quality as follows:

> Most of them are stamped with the Puritanism of their author,
> than which nothing can be more alien to the sonnet sequences of
> the sixteenth and seventeenth centuries. Instead of showing the
> light grace, the richness and ornate beauty, of the earlier type,
> they are distinguished by vigor, dignity, and exaltation. They are
> more sonorous and direct, they have what Wordsworth termed
> "republican austerity," they are restrained and classic; in a word,
> they are Miltonic, for they are marked with the characteristics
> that distinguish Milton the man and the poet. Yet . . . they lack
> the grace, loveliness, and sheer beauty of Shakespeare's qua-
> torzains.[12]

They came, nevertheless, at a time when the sheer
loveliness of grace needed something to keep it from
melting down into broken sighs and tears in hands
less capable than Shakespeare's; when England needed
"soul animating strains" though they must be "alas,
too few!" Accordingly, when Milton's influence
reached the poets of the eighteenth and early nineteenth centuries, sonnets were benefited both as to
form and content.

Finally, in addition to enlarging the scope of themes
and strengthening the texture of the sonnet, Milton
was to bring to it a new structural conception. Going
far beyond the mere manipulation of rime schemes,
which had been the Elizabethans' principal contribution, he was to give to the stiffened verses a flexibility
seldom felt in the early examples of the form. As we
have noted, in the Petrarchan sonnet a pause at the
end of the eighth verse was normal, and frequently
this was anticipated by another at the end of the
opening quatrain. Similiar pauses became characteristic also in the Elizabethan sonnet, and both
Spenser and Shakespeare adhered rigidly to end-stop-

ping at the quatrain junctions. Normally, too, in
both the Italian and English use the verse had been
maintained as a unit, and seldom admitted a medial
pause stronger than a comma. In other words, if the
thought of a verse was permitted to run over, the
enjambment would carry through to the end of the
next verse, or beyond that to the end of the next following. Naturally, this constant reaching for the ends
of verses tended towards monotony and was one of
the basic factors in stiffening an already structurally
rigid form.

Probably the most important innovation made by
Milton was in permitting greater numbers of enjambment verses, even at the divisional points, and more
frequent and pronounced medial pauses.* In doing
so he gave full play to the scope of the heroic meter,
exactly as he was to do with the same meter in his
blank-verse poems. Yet it was not mere license; there
is always an appropriateness of relationship between
form and content, and an artistic justification for his
use. He was to describe its structural principle later,
for the basis of his blank-verse defense is equally applicable to his sonnet technique. Granting the necessity
of rime in the form, it is still possible to conceive of
there being a "musical delight" subtler and richer than
that provided by the "jingling sound of like endings,"
a music "which consists only in apt numbers, fit
quantity of syllables, and the sense variously drawn
out from one verse into another."[13]

In his realization of this principle, and in over-
coming the uniformity which had too frequently re-
solved itself into mere monotony, Milton was to
achieve, as no one had done before, the goal of variety

---

*Of the nineteen sonnets (including the caudated example) Havens [op. cit.,
pp. 438-84] finds that six omit the strong pause after the first quatrain; nine
after the octave, six being run-on at this point; and that there are twenty-eight
strong pauses within the lines, eleven of which mark the ends of sentences.

within uniformity. He was also to set a precedent for beauty and flexibility of phrasing that has been characteristic of the form since his day.

Because he thus overcame precedent Milton has been frowned upon for the degree to which he breaks from Petrarch.[14] But one must realize that there were other writers of the sonnet to whom the poet may have turned for authority. As J. S. Smart suggests, Milton revered the classical unities in the drama, but apparently did not regard the sonnet as bound by stringent laws since it was a modern poetic form. One should not, therefore, judge him by legislation of which he had never heard. And Smart points out further that it is unfair to criticize the poet by comparing him with Petrarch alone, for in Giovanni della Casa (d. 1556), a copy of whose sonnets Milton purchased in 1629, is found a poet who deliberately broke from smoothness and regularity and brought the entire quatorzain into a closer-knit fabric. Casa's "aim is to produce new effects by some sudden and striking departure from the familiar flow of language and verse. His sentences ignore the bounds of meter, passing imperceptibly from line to line, and ending abruptly where an ear attuned to Petrarch's modulation might least have expected; the close, which may occur at any point, being weighty and emphatic."[15]

6

Spenser cannot be said to have influenced the eighteenth-century sonnet in any appreciable degree, and Shakespeare received only a minor following until the close of the period. But, after the decades (1660-1740) in which writers "sway'd about upon a rocking horse" in perfecting the heroic couplet and only thirteen are known to have used the quatorzain, there came to Milton abundant recognition. For when, about 1750, opposition to the couplet came in—when poets realized that the artificiality of the metronome could no longer be substituted for the freedom demanded by the creative mind—it was emulation of Milton's quatorzains that marked the sonnet revival and hastened its development.

The number of eighteenth-century sonnets (see Table III[17]) examined by R. D. Havens is significant when it is recalled that the period 1740-1800 has been supposed a comparative desert with respect to the

TABLE III*

EIGHTEENTH CENTURY SONNET DEVELOPMENT

	Petrarchan	Shakespearean	Spenserian	Irregular
1740-60 (20 years)	73	0	7	20
1760-80 (20 years)	130	27	2	348
1780-90 (10 years)	234	154	7	448
1790-1800 (10 years)	199	270	1	582
Total	636	451	17	1398

form. But the evidence of numbers does not necessarily furnish the corollary that critical interest was equally apparent, and of the latter there was little in this period. Havens suggests five typical groups of those who gave varying degrees of consideration to the sonnet: first, those who disliked all quatorzains (Samuel Johnson); second, those who admired all that were passable regardless of structure (William Hayley and Sir Egerton Brydges); third, those who were averse to the regular forms, preferring the irregular sonnets dealing with sentimental melancholy (Coleridge and Mrs. Charlotte Smith); fourth, ardent Milton enthusiasts who looked askance at any but what they considered truly Petrarchan (Anna Seward);

*Havens' note on this table is important: "... the first column contains only poems that conform to a strict, probably an over-strict, interpretation of the phrase 'Petrarchan rime-scheme,' one that would exclude a considerable number of sonnets written by Milton and Petrarch himself.... Assuming that one-sixth of the irregular quatorzains were intended to be and in the main are legitimate, we should have about 870 Petrarchesque, as against 17 Spenserian, 450 Shakespearean, and 1165 irregular quatorzains."

and fifth, by far the largest group, those who probably
held no opinion at all.

While the work of most of these writers remained
unpublished for years and, being practically unknown,
could have exerted little influence on contemporaries,
the possibility of its having been available to poets of
the early nineteenth century, and to Keats in particular, makes it desirable to indicate something of the
specific ideas relating to the form. A series of brief
quotations showing first the general attitude towards
the sonnet as a poem, without consideration of pattern, and second the opinion relating to structure, may
serve this purpose; in any event it will be clear from
the following that much of the commentary must be
ascribed either to ignorance, devotion to Milton, or
opposition *per se* to anything resembling a sonnet:[18]

Milton . . . was, we believe, the first Englishman that was
induced to attempt the sonnet in the language of our island.
[*Monthly Review* of 1797]

The strongest act of Parliament that could be framed, would
fail to compel readers into their service. [George Stevens in
omitting the sonnets from his edition of Shakespeare, 1793]

The sonnets of Shakespeare are buried beneath a load of obscurity and quaintness; nor does there issue a single ray of light
to quicken, or to warm the heavy mass. . . . His last editor has, I
think, acted with greater judgement, in forebearing to obtrude
such crude effects upon the public eye: for where is the utility
of propagating compositions which no one can endure to read?
[Nathan Drake in *Literary Hours*, 1798]

It is scarcely necessary to say that he [Spenser] has completely
failed. In his long series of sonnets, the critic will recognize many
of the trifling conceits of the Italian, but find little to recompense
the trouble of research. [*Ibid.*]

Until the time of Drummond we can advance slender claim
to any degree of elegance in this species of versification. . . . In too
many instances . . . our early sonnets abound with sentiments so

hyperbolically uttered, and resemblances so extravagantly and uncouthly drawn, as must necessarily render them disgusting to any but a rude or uncultivated taste. [George Henderson in *Petrarcha,* 1803]

Other writers preferred to indicate their attitude towards Shakespeare and Spenser by omission, rather than by stated expression. Miss Seward, though she wrote extensively, mentions them only once. Henry White in his remarks in the *Gentleman's Magazine* (1786) fails to mention them. Indeed, the first who seems to have cared for the sonnets of Shakespeare with anything like affection was William Blake, "the first poet of the century with a real gift of song," and we find that "Shakespeare's Venus and Adonis, Tarquin and Lucrece, and his Sonnets" are described by B. H. Malkin in 1806 as "poems, now little read, [which] were favourite studies of Mr. Blake's early days."

But if Spenser and Shakespeare were ignored or opposed by eighteenth-century sonneteers, Milton was more favorably received. Samuel Johnson, as might be expected, was cold: "Of the best it can only be said that they are not bad, and perhaps only the eighth and twenty-first are truly entitled to this slender commendation." But Miss Seward is attracted by their "hardness" and "energetic plainness," comparing them to "the pointed and craggy rock, the grace of which is its roughness." And others, as we shall see, turned to Milton as their authority in matters of structure. At best, however, one can only say that, while a few poets and many poetasters were writing sonnets during this period, there is little evidence that any genuine feeling for the possibilities or beauties of the quatorzain, or of the extant examples, was felt. It was scarcely an age tempered to such appreciation, and it is not surprising that "among the persons using the form between 1740 and 1820 were all the poets of note (and many long since forgotten) who were inclined to romanticism, but none of those opposed to it."[19]

That there was scarcely more attention paid to the question of form in the sonnet will be evident from a corresponding set of typical comments. Most of the writers were satisfied merely to imitate the models offered by Milton or Shakespeare without inquiry as to the artistic basis for the structure, or any consistency in the relationship between their theory and practice. Thus Capel Lofft could vigorously urge Kirk White to use the legitimate (Petrarchan) form, in a sonnet which, despite its author's having translated many Italian sonnets and edited an anthology of quatorzains, has a run-on at the end of the eighth verse and a rime scheme *abbaababcddcee*, indicating clearly that attempts to make the canon rigid had not yet arrived. And many of the extant commentaries show this seemingly confused attitude, or limit themselves to single features of structure determined by precedent rather than principle:

Of Milton's English sonnets, only that to Oliver Cromwell ends with a couplet; but that single instance is sufficient precedent. However, in three out of his five Italian ones, the two concluding lines rhime to each other. [*Gentleman's Magazine*, 1786]

The little poems [approximations to the Shakespearean] which are here called sonnets, have, I believe, no very just claim to that title. [Charlotte Smith in preface to *Elegiac Sonnets*, 1784]

... two stanzas ... of four verses each; and two of three; the eight verses being all in three [*sic*] rhimes. [*Encyclopedia Britannica*, editions 1 to 6, 1771-1824]*

It is to end with some pretty, ingenious thought: the close must be particularly beautiful, or the *sonnet* is naught. [*Chamber's Cyclopedia*, 1728 and 1752]

---

*One must feel less harsh towards the first editions of this work when he reads in the latest (14th) edition of the *Britannica* that the Spenserian rime scheme is *ababbcbccdcdcc*, and that the Shakespearean is *ababcdcdccgg*.

... correct, simple, not aiming at points or turns, in the phrase and structure rather ancient, for the most part of a grave, or even of a melancholy cast; formed in short upon the model of the Italians of the good age, and of their imitators among us, Spenser [*sic*] and Milton. [Thomas Edwards in describing his own work]

The fabrick of a sonnet however adapted to the Italian language, has never succeeded in ours. ... Milton, Madam, was a genius that could cut a Collossus from a rock; but could not carve heads upon cherry stones. [Samuel Johnson]

I confined myself to fourteen lines because fourteen lines seemed best adapted to unity of sentiment. I thought nothing about the strict Italian model; the verses naturally flowed in unpremeditated harmony, as my ear directed. [William Lysle Bowles on his own sonnets]

It has been the fashion of late to despise sonnets, more especially those, which, on account of the technical repetition, and contexture, of the rhymes, are called legitimate. [Sir Egerton Brydges in *Poems*, 1807]

These are but typical illustrations of the meagerness of any knowledge or care in regard to sonnet structure, and it is not surprising that the great mass of those considered by Havens should fall into the "irregular" grouping. There were, naturally, a few purists even in that day, but their insistence was mainly on adherence to rime scheme, and most frequently on the Petrarchan, to the exclusion of Shakespeare and all who imitated him. Miss Anna Seward, herself a prolific writer and staunch defender of Milton, offered what is probably the closest approximation to a canon in her various comments on the form. Condensed and summarized, the following points are typical of her theory:

1. There should be one thought, regularly pursued to the close.
2. The rhythm should be that of blank verse, with the pauses coming within rather than at the ends of verses.

3. Any order of rimes is permissible, but in the octave the number should be limited to two.

4. A concluding couplet is permissible, but a new or detached thought should not be permitted at that point, since "Brilliance, or epigrammatic turn or point, belong not to that species of composition."

5. Most important are dignity and energetic plainness.

6. It should be "grave and severe," have "strength and majesty," and "rather an elevated simplicity than that Popean smoothness and polish."[20]

The source of most of these ideas, as Miss Seward herself admitted, was an admiration of Milton's sonnets, but since her poems and letters were not published until the two years following her death (1809) her eighteenth-century influence was limited to a circle of friends. Her popularity in the early decades of the nineteenth century, however, makes her ideas worthy of our attention—and the nature of those ideas was to lead away from characteristically Elizabethan subject matter and form, and to emphasize those that approximated the Miltonic. Henry F. Cary, in his commentary on Miss Seward's work, interprets her conception of the difference between the sonnets of Milton and Spenser as follows:

A distinction should be made between the Miltonic and Spenseric sonnet; the first may be used on grave and sublime, the latter on tender subjects; the diction of the former ought to be elevated and yet simple, and should require a sort of majesty by the pauses and breaks peculiar to blank verse; that of the latter should be neat, polished, and smooth throughout.[21]

It is this greater flexibility that will be noted as one of the principal characteristics in the sonnets of early nineteenth-century poets, as well as in those of Milton, when they are compared with the sonnets of Spenser and Shakespeare.

From the foregoing one obvious conclusion may be

drawn relative to the sonnets of Keats. Had he been entirely dependent for his knowledge of the form on the available sonnets and commentary of eighteenth-century writers, there would be scarcely any standards by which his work could be judged. Fortunately, however, two contemporaries,* Wordsworth and Leigh Hunt—the first of whom made extensive use of the sonnet and emphasized an important English variant, and the second of whom held definite and influential ideas as to its structure and form—were in some degree to stabilize the eighteenth-century inconsistencies and pave the way for Keats's own Petrarchan attempts.

7

It was not until Wordsworth had mastered his technique in other poetic forms that he found any interest in the sonnet. To be exact, it was during the afternoon of May 21, 1802, that Dorothy read aloud (is poetry ever truly such until it is so read?) the sonnets of Milton, and her brother, who already knew them well, suddenly realized their full harmony and "republican austerity" as if these qualities had only now become a part of the lines. The moment, an important one in the history of the form, is recorded by the poet:

One afternoon . . . my sister read to me the sonnets of Milton. I had long been well acquainted with them, but I was particularly struck on that occasion with the dignified simplicity and majestic harmony that runs through most of them—in character so totally different from the Italian, and still more so from Shakespeare's fine sonnets. I took fire, if I may be allowed to say so, and produced three sonnets the same afternoon, the first I ever wrote except an irregular one at school.[22]

*Of the others, Coleridge's sonnets are quite irregular. Byron wrote only a half dozen and Shelley scarcely more, all quite irregular in form. None of these seems to have influenced Keats, while his early admiration of Wordsworth and Hunt would naturally lead to emulation.

Indeed, before that afternoon Wordsworth had considered the sonnet "egregiously absurd," especially as to its structure; after it he was to become England's most prolific sonnet writer, with no less than 523 titles. The impetus of his "taking fire" resulted in nineteen quatorzains before the end of the year, many of them among his finest: "Composed Upon Westminster Bridge," "On the Extinction of the Venetian Republic," "To Toussaint L'Ouverture," "London, 1802," and "It is a beauteous evening, calm and free" being in the number.

That the sonnets of Wordsworth make such a distinct advance over those of the closing decades of the eighteenth century may be ascribed in large part to the fact that it was Milton, and not Wordsworth's early contemporaries, to whom he turned for guidance. At first there was to be found much of the austerity of mood, the similarity in themes, the blank-verse type of structural flexibility, and the characteristic vocative opening used by most of Milton's imitators. But after mastering the form a change can be noted, a shift to the less imitative, quieter, more calmly restrained mood so characteristic of the Lake poet, and to an even freer use of the form; though his theory, where expressed, is confused and frequently inconsistent with his practice.

But there are two distinct differences between Milton and Wordsworth as writers of the Petrarchan sonnet. The first is the inclusion, by Wordsworth, of nature (and, frequently coupled with it, the celebration of places of interest) as a subject for sonnet treatment. Only in the quatorzain beginning "O Nightingale, that on yon bloomy spray" does Milton make any such use, and even here it is secondary to his love theme. Since, however, Wordsworth had been developing his philosophy of nature in other poems for many years, he would, naturally, not hesitate to make such themes a part of his newly realized verse form. But this in itself was not an innovation so far as the sonnet was concerned. For with all of the attention paid by the late eighteenth century to melancholy, grief, and other typically pre-Romantic themes, the widely spreading "return" to nature had found a place in the heterogeneous assortment of sonnet literature.

Thomas Warton was among the first to bring the sonnet into the service of nature and interesting locale, as his "Sonnet Written at Stonehenge" and "Sonnet to the River Lodon" testify. He was followed by many others, among the few of importance being John Bampfylde, who dealt almost exclusively with nature, and Mrs. Charlotte Smith, who was regarded by many, including Coleridge, as a model in the use of the form.

But no writer before Wordsworth was more influential than was William Lysle Bowles who, appealing particularly to poets (Coleridge made more than forty handwritten copies to distribute as gifts[23]), did much to establish the form as a medium for recording visits to places of interest and for descriptions or interpretations of natural phenomena. Such titles as "At Tynemouth Priory," "The Bells, Ostend," "Bamborough Castle," "Approach of Summer," "Evening," and "Dover Cliffs," are typical and have their counterparts in many of the sonnets of Wordsworth, Coleridge, and Keats. As we shall see below, Bowles's influence was largely in the field of subject matter, and in his use of form he was closer to the Elizabethans than to his contemporaries.

The introduction of themes relating to nature, or to places of legendary, historical, or personal interest, represents one of the principal contributions of the eighteenth century to the sonnet. Uncertain as the writers of the time may have been regarding the characteristics and possibilities of the form, and imperfect as were their attempts to imitate Milton and his predecessors, there remains the distinctly practical use to which they put the quatorzain. The Elizabethans had spun their poems from the stuff of their inner consciousness, and had burdened them with conceits, familiar images, and the clichés of sentiment and language. From this to the precision of utterance, the care in word choice, and the individual expression of definite ideas whose origin was the political, religious, social, and personal world about him, Milton was the guide. It remained then, after the urban interests of the pseudo-classic period began to give way to the renewal of interest in nature, for the eighteenth century to widen still more the range of themes suited to the form. And though the expression was at first handicapped by technical incompetency, it offered a precedent, and it is in the degree to which Wordsworth followed this influence that he is to be distinguished, in the matter of themes, from Milton.

As to form, Wordsworth emulated the general freedom of Milton as regarded the heroic verse, but went even beyond when difficulties arose concerning rime; for in nearly half of his total number of sonnets he included a third rime in the octave, giving the pattern *abbaacca*, a pattern used earlier by Drummond and Bowles.[24] Of this octave William Sharp has written:

There have been some fine sonnets written with the introduction of a third rhyme-sound into the octave (the terminations of the sixth and seventh lines), and there can be no doubt that if this were equally satisfactory to the ear, a still greater and most valuable expansion would be given to the English sonnet; but to the sensitive ear, especially sensitive among Italians, it is as out of place as some new strain is in a melody that is already in itself amply sufficient, and that loses in effect by the alien introduction.[25]

On the other hand, the scarcity of rimes in English, or the desirability of variety in a poem as short and compact as the sonnet, might reasonably justify the third rime sound. The presence of the including *a* rimes should serve to maintain the "melody," and if a slight variation in its supporting harmony is introduced it need not necessarily result in discord. The final test must, of course, always be the poet's command of his craftsmanship, or musicianship.

In the sestet, too, Wordsworth generally maintained the same freedom. While there are only four instances of the closing couplet in the first six years of his sonnet writing, he was later to become more lax, and the wide variety of his patterns has already been noted (Table II).

Following Milton again, Wordsworth, in theory at least, exercised freedom in the omission of the pause between octave and sestet. Apparently ignorant of della Casa, Milton's source, Wordsworth ascribed this characteristic in Milton to the latter's desire to give the sonnet a less artificial organization and greater unity. As late as 1833, in a letter that is probably significant of the state of general knowledge regarding the sonnet in the early nineteenth century, Wordsworth writes:

Though I have written so many, I have scarcely made up my own mind upon the subject. It should seem that the sonnet, like every other legitimate composition, ought to have a beginning, a middle, and an end; in other words, to consist of three parts. . . . But the frame of meter adopted by the Italians . . . seems to be— if not arbitrary—best fitted to a division of the senses into two parts, of eight and six lines each. Milton, however, has not submitted to this; in the better half of his sonnets the sense does not close with the rhyme at the eighth line, but overflows into the second portion of the meter. Now it has struck me that this is not done merely to gratify the ear by variety and freedom of sound, but also to aid in giving that pervading sense of intense unity in which the excellence of the sonnet has always seemed to me mainly to consist. Instead of looking at this composition as a piece of architecture, making a whole out of three parts, I have been much in the habit of preferring the image of an orbicular body,—a sphere or a dew-drop. . . . I am well aware that a sonnet will often be found excellent, where the beginning, the middle, and the end are distinctly marked, and also where it is distinctly separated into two parts.[26]

But, as frequently, Wordsworth's practice only partly supported his theory, and in the fifty-six sonnets of the 1807 volumes Hutchinson finds thirty-four with full octave stop and a turn in the sestet; only seven with no pause at the octave, nor any subdivision corresponding to the quatrains and tercets (the "orbicular" type?); and fifteen which have the pause occurring in the middle of the eighth or ninth verse rather than at the end of the octave.[27]

Thus Wordsworth, with Milton, did much to free the sonnet from the traditional characteristics of the Elizabethans, and from the sentimentality, melancholy, and triviality of the eighteenth century. He used it as a medium for his thought rather than as a pattern to be served, and treated in it not only the stuff of his dreams, but also the scenes of his Lake District and the many facets of the changing world about him.

By 1816 Wordsworth had published 109 sonnets— any or all of which Keats might have read—a number large enough and important enough to be influential. Keats's early admiration for the older writer is well known,* and it may have been this in part that de-

*Keats writes to Haydon [letter 6]: "The idea of your sending it [Sonnet, "Great spirits . . . "] to Wordsworth put me out of breath—you know with what reverence I would send my well-wishes to him."

layed the youthful poet in his attempt at the Shake-spearean form (since Wordsworth adheres invariably to the Petrarchan), although the fact that Hunt had tried the pattern in his *Juvenilia* and apparently abandoned it would probably suggest his as the final influence. Similarities in themes will be found in the sonnets of Wordsworth and Keats, and certain detailed structural parallels suggesting influence will be noted below. On the other hand, if Keats were imitating, one would almost certainly expect to find the obvious *abbaacca* octave pattern, which does not occur in Keats's extant sonnets.

The answer to this discrepancy is probably to be found in Keats's relationship with Leigh Hunt, who is accused by the poet at one time of being "much dis-posed to dissect and anatomize any trip or slip I may have made."[28] Wordsworth was admired from afar, but from Hunt, Keats could receive suggestions; with him he could talk, write competitive sonnets, and come under the influence of his friend's general critical theory. Of such theory Hunt had a great deal, as his writing attests, and in regard to the sonnet his theory was, some years after Keats's death, or-ganized into a unified essay, showing an understanding of the form never exhibited by Wordsworth.

8

The enthusiasm with which Keats became a mem-ber of the Hunt circle, and the resulting general in-fluence on the younger poet's work have been too frequently emphasized to require repetition here, but too often only the more obvious aspects of the rela-tionship have been considered. In diction and in weak-ness of imagery he who runs may find abundant paral-lels. Keats's admiration of "Rimini" is attested by his

sonnet on that poem; it is likewise clear that he carried
the weakness of it into his own work. But there have
been few objective attempts (and none for the sonnet)
to determine whether or not this influence went beyond the easily imitated characteristics and into the
more subtle technical elements. To do so for the
sonnets will be one part of the later sections of this
work. Here we may pause long enough to note certain other significant points at which the two poets
are brought together through their interest in the
form.

It is in the sonnet, one of the earliest extant,[29] that
Keats first shows his admiration for the imprisoned
Hunt, whose liberation occasioned the poem. Keats's
first published work, the sonnet "To Solitude," was
printed by Hunt in *The Examiner* and served to introduce the young poet both to the public and the publisher. It drew from Hunt the following comment on
the samples of Keats's work from which it was
chosen: "I shall never forget the impression made
upon me by the exuberant specimens of genuine
though young poetry that were laid before me."[30]
Later, when Keats had joined the circle, the sonnet
form was to offer an excuse for passing delightful
competitive hours, and "On the Grasshopper and the
Cricket," published with Hunt's version in *The Examiner*,[31] and "To the Nile" resulted from such pas-
time. Hunt wrote a sonnet to Keats, and the latter
poet has addressed, or referred to, the other no less
than ten times in the sonnets, representative titles
being "Written on the Day that Mr. Leigh Hunt
Left Prison," "On Receiving a Laurel Crown from
Leigh Hunt," "To Leigh Hunt, Esq.," (the dedicatory
sonnet of the 1817 volume), and "On Leigh Hunt's
Poem 'The Story of Rimini.' "[32]

More than this, Hunt and Keats were made the butts

of critical attacks because of their sonnet proclivities. Keats's sonnet containing the line (referring to Hunt) "He of the rose, the violet, the spring," became in effect the official Cockney poem, by an "amiable but infatuated bardling."[33] *Blackwoods Magazine* in 1819 parodied the Cockney conceits and mannerisms in a facetious bit of prose on sonnet writing and in a "Sonnet on Myself," the target of their satire being evident. The same magazine in 1821 described Hunt as "The whining milk-sop sonneteer of the *Examiner*" and pictured him as "sipping tea, playing whist, and writing sonnets." And the "Sonnet on Receiving a Crown of Ivy from Keats" was particularly attacked with the suggestion that "a blister clapped on his head" would be more appropriate.[34]

With such mutual interest centering around sonnet activity it would indeed be surprising if the two poets did not discuss the form they were writing. Hunt, as we have seen, had used it since his juvenile attempts at composition, and his criticisms of Keats's and others' poems show that his theory was definite and reasonably complete. More than this, it was a theory such as might, and did, influence the younger man, to what degree our later comparisons will show.

The organized expression of Hunt's opinion and theory concerning the form is given in "An Essay on the Cultivation, History, and Varieties of the Species of Poem Called the Sonnet," written as an introductory section to *The Book of the Sonnet*, a collaboration with S. Adams Lee. The aim of the work was to present English and American sonnets of the highest order, and to indicate the phases of development named in the title of Hunt's essay. Published posthumously in 1867, the essay represents Hunt's mature thought regarding the form; but the opinions are different from those held in the days of association with Keats only in their more complete organization, and are, therefore, fully indicative of the ideas Keats himself may have received from, or shared with, Hunt.

In the "Essay" Hunt writes of the desirability of cultivating the sonnet, outlines its nature and properties, traces its Italian backgrounds (expressing a preference for Dante over Petrarch because the grace of the former is preferable to the elegance of the latter), describes the more important of its hybrid patterns, finds little favorable to say concerning the English modifications, and closes by naming Keats's "On First Looking Into Chapman's Homer" as the finest of all sonnets in the English language. With certain aspects of Hunt's thought the foregoing pages have already dealt. There remains for consideration here his "summary of the conditions requisite to a perfect sonnet." Of these conditions the critic has listed thirteen:

1. It must be a legitimate sonnet after the proper Italian fashion; that is to say, with but two rimes in the octave, and not more than three in the sestet.

2. It must confine itself to one leading idea, thought, or feeling.

3. It must treat this one leading idea, thought, or feeling, in such a manner as to leave in the reader's mind no sense of irrelevancy or insufficiency.

4. It must not have a speck of obscurity.

5. It must not have a forced rime.*

6. It must not have a superfluous word.*

7. It must not have a word too little; that is to say, an omission of a word or words, for the sake of convenience.

8. It must not have a word out of its place.

9. It must have no very long word, or any other that tends to lessen the number of accents, and so weaken the verse.

10. Its rimes must be properly varied and contrasted, and not beat upon the same vowel,—a fault too common with very good sonnets. It must not say, for instance, *rime, tide, abide, crime;* or

---

*Hunt's principal objection to Spenser is that "he has a great many superfluous words" and "often forces his rimes." [*Imagination and Fancy,* p. 62.]

play, gain, refrain, way; but contrast *i* with *o*, or with some other strongly opposed vowel, and treat every vowel on the same principle.

11. Its music, throughout, must be as varied as it is suitable; more or less strong, or sweet, according to the subject; but never weak or monotonous, unless monotony itself be the effect intended.

12. It must increase, or, at all events, not decline, in interest, to its close.

13. The close must be equally impressive and unaffected; not epigrammatic, unless where the subject warrants it, or where point of that kind is desirable; but simple, conclusive, and satisfactory; strength being paramount, where such elevation is natural, otherwise on a level with serenity; flowing in calmness, or grand in manifestation of power withheld.*

An analysis of these thirteen points will show that basically Hunt is concerned with three phases of sonnet structure. First is his advocacy of the Italian form. We have already noted his objection to the Spenserian pattern and his comment on the "unartistical" nature of the Shakespearean. The Petrarchan he calls the legitimate, and there is no reason to believe, with M. R. Ridley, that Keats would consider either of the other forms under this title.† We know that it was not until late in 1817 that Keats turned from the Petrarchan to the Shakespearean form, and that in all

---

*Hunt, "Essay," pp. 14-15. The reasonableness of Hunt's canon will be evident. William Sharp, in his essay on the sonnet (1886) practically re-states Hunt's points. It is interesting to compare such an approach with that of a purist like T. W. H. Crosland [*The English Sonnet*, pp. 88-97], whose twenty-one points become almost a *reductio ad absurdum* of sonnet legislation. Leigh Hunt anticipated the danger and futility of such rigid legislation in the following statement: "That such a system could never prevail over the manifest temptations to be more free and easy, need hardly be observed. The sonnet was too obvious a resource for expressing any emotion whatsoever, to be restricted to formalities so pedantic; and accordingly it finally obeyed no laws in general but those that are essential to all good poetry, with the exception of such as were to render it what it was, and to secure for it that completeness, and that freedom from blemish, which alone can render a small thing precious." ["Essay," p. 11.]

† Ridley contends [*Keats' Craftsmanship*, p. 203] that in view of Keats's attitude towards Shakespeare he would apply "legitimate" to the Shakespearean pattern. Only ignorance of the history of the sonnet and its criticism would account for such a statement. Not only in Hunt but generally the Italian was referred to as the legitimate.

his Italian sonnets he uses the pattern characterized by Hunt; this, too, in the face of his knowledge of Wordsworth's modification. Apparently Hunt's influence had to be on the wane before Keats turned to the Shakespearean pattern.

Secondly, Hunt is concerned with the artistic unity by which the material of the sonnet is developed. Economy of expression, advance to a desirable close, and appropriateness of relationship between form and content, represent the burden of many of these points. It should be noted that his emphasis is on one *leading* thought; he does not deny the possibility of balance between idea and idea, or contrast in ideas for emphasis, but asks only that there shall be that desirable center of attention required of all artistic production. That this second phase of his theory is not limited to the mature thought of the "Essay," and that it is undoubtedly the sort of thing he would emphasize in Keats's presence, is shown by his comments on the poems of Keats during the latter's lifetime. Since the points made under this grouping relate to poetry in general and not particularly to the sonnet as a form, we may assume the statement as to Hunt's first acquaintance with the verses of Keats—"exuberant specimens of genuine though young poetry"—to mean that from the beginning the younger poet evidenced, for him, that artistic unity which would be synonymous with "genuine" poetry. But Hunt could be more definite than this, both in favoring and in adversely criticizing the poet. His dicta concerning obscurity, the best word, and the sonnet close, are all summed up in his comment relating to the sonnet "On First Looking Into Chapman's Homer":

The rest of the composition, with the exception of a little vagueness in calling the regions of poetry "the realms of gold," we do not hesitate to pronounce excellent, especially the last six lines. The word *swims* is complete; and the whole conclusion is equally powerful and quiet.[35]

In such a statement Hunt practically epitomizes the sonnet theory he was to express later in more detail in the "Essay." And in July, 1817, he was to voice a dissatisfaction that Keats, in the 1817 volume, had not exercised sufficient restraint and unity of impression. He finds

> . . . a tendency to notice everything too indiscriminately and without an eye to natural proportion and effect. . . . There is a superabundance of detail, which, though not so wanting, of course, in power of perception, is as faulty and unseasonable sometimes as common-place. It depends upon circumstances, whether we are to consider ourselves near enough, as it were, to the subject we are describing to grow microscopical upon it. A person basking in a landscape, for instance, and a person riding through it, are in two very different situations for the exercise of their eyesight; and even where the license is most allowable, care must be taken not to give to small things and great, to nice detail and to general feeling, the same proportion of effect. Errors of this kind in poetry answer to a want of perspective in painting, and of a due distribution of light and shade.[36]

Finally, in his canon Hunt gives particular detail to his consideration of devices for sound. This is not surprising when one remembers that the poet, publisher, and critic was likewise an excellent musician and a capable pianist. But he seems to have been better able to detect such flaws in the work of others than to correct them in his own, for we shall see below that the point on which he is most specific— the contrasting of vowel sounds in the rimes—finds many exceptions in his own work, as it does in that of Keats. This inconsistency suggests that it was only late in life that the more subtle vowel balance became a part of his theory; but that he was sensitive to other sound effects, and emphasized them with respect to the poetry of Keats, may be easily shown. In one instance, particularly, an important change seems to have been made by Keats as a result of Hunt's criticism. The published version of the "Chapman's Homer" sonnet had the lines:

> That deep-brow'd Homer ruled as his demesne;
> Yet could I never judge what men could mean . . .

Clarke says the poet changed the second of these lines because it was "bald and too simply wondering."[37] Amy Lowell suggests in addition that Keats must have been conscious of the unfortunate repetition of *could,* of the awkwardly repeated consonants and vowels, and of the identical quality in the *demesne-mean* rime. Miss Lowell calls this version of the sonnet a "first draft."[38] That it was not in the sense in which she seems to imply is indicated by the fact that it is the published version in *The Examiner* for December 1, 1816 (it had been written in October), and that Hunt wrote of it on that date: "In the following sonnet there is one incorrect rhyme [*demesne-mean*], which might be easily altered, but which shall serve in the meantime as a peace offering to the rhyming critics." And it was clearly after this criticism that the line was changed.*

As to general music blended with the rhythmical movement of lines, Hunt seems to be in agreement with Milton that "apt numbers, fit quantity of syllables, and the sense variously drawn out from one verse into another" should be the determining factors. In commenting on the 1817 volume he criticizes the indiscriminate nature of the subject matter, then continues:

---

*Hunt was always keenly sensitive to rime sounds. *Cf.* his criticism of Pope [*Table Talk,* p. 128] and his discussion of a variant passage in "Kubla Khan" [*Imagination and Fancy,* p. 261].

Mr. Keats's other fault, the one in versification, arises from a similar cause, that of contradicting over-zealously the fault on the opposite side [the over-smoothness of Pope?]. It is this which provokes him now and then into mere roughness and discords for their own sake, not for that of variety and contrasted harmony.[39]

And in the light of the principles he so staunchly advocated, there is something of the satisfaction found by the teacher for his pupil as Hunt takes his leave of the 1820 volume:

The author's versification is now perfected, the exuberance of imagination restrained, and a calm power, the surest and loftiest of all power, takes place of the impatient workings of the younger god within him. . . . Mr. Keats undoubtedly takes his seat with the oldest and best of our living poets.[40]

The foregoing quotations and discussion lead to the conclusion that the sonnet theory of Leigh Hunt was not alone the product of his later life, but that the ideas concerning sonnet legislation, as expressed in the "Essay," had been an actual part of his poetic thought and criticism during that formative period when Keats was writing under his influence. Their close association at that time, and the early admiration Keats felt for his friend, might lead, without this corroboration, to the assumption that the neophyte would emulate the more experienced writer. With the definite support of the above and later evidence there can be little question that Hunt's theories and prejudices were taken over by Keats in the early period of influence.*

---

*The relationship between Hunt's theory of the sonnet and his theory of general versification, which likewise must have influenced Keats, will be suggested by the following point summary condensed from "In Answer to the Question, What is Poetry" [*Imagination and Fancy*, pp. 31ff.]

1. Verse should be modulated by variety in uniformity.

2. Verse is the final proof to the poet that his mastery over his art is complete. It is the shutting up of his powers in *measureful* content; the answer of form to his spirit; of strength and ease to his guidance.

3. Every poet, then, is a versifier; every fine poet an excellent one; and he is best whose verse exhibits the greatest amount of strength, sweetness, straightforwardness, unsuperfluousness, variety, and oneness; oneness, that is to say, consistency in the general impression, metrical and moral; and variety, or every pertinent diversity of tone and rhythm, in the process. Strength is the

As to the petty quarrels between the two, there is no very strong reason to suppose that their effects, and not the maturing of his own powers, changed the literary relationship of Keats towards Hunt. Keats himself was by nature too friendly to remain antagonistic for long. True, he speaks disparagingly of Hunt's "self-delusion" in flattering himself "into the idea of being a great poet"; he mistrusts Hunt's motives and feels that the latter is taking too much credit for his (Keats's) poetry; he accuses Hunt of being greatly disposed to "dissect and anatomise any trip or slip I may have made"; he assigns him to the "tribe of Manasseh," and calls him "vain, egotistical and disgusting in matters of taste and morals"; he classes him with Wordsworth in the matter of "idle conversation"; and he refuses to room longer with the Hunt

---

muscle of verse, and shows itself in the number and force of the marked syllables. Unexpected locations of accent double this force.

4. The abuse of strength is harshness and heaviness; the reverse is weakness. Weakness in versification is want of accent and emphasis. It generally accompanies prosaicalness, and is the consequence of weak thoughts, and of the affectation of a certain well-bred enthusiasm.

5. Sweetness is the smoothness of grace and delicacy [he illustrates by assonance].

6. Straightforwardness is the flow of words in their natural order, free alike from mere prose, and from those inversions to which bad poets recur in order to escape the charge of prose, but chiefly to accommodate their rimes.

7. Unsuperfluousness is rather a matter of style in general, than of the sound and order of words.

8. Variety of versification consists in whatsoever can be done for the prevention of monotony, by diversity of stops and cadences, distribution of emphasis, and retardation and acceleration of time; for the whole real secret of versification is a musical secret, and is not attainable to any vital effect save by the ear of genius. The same time and quantity which are occasioned by the spiritual part of this secret, thus become its formal ones,—not feet and syllables, long and short, iambics or trochees, which are the reduction of it to its *less* than dry bones. You might get, for instance, not only ten and eleven, but thirteen and fourteen syllables into a rhyming, as well as blank, heroical verse, if time and feeling permitted; and in irregular measure this is often done; just as musicians put twenty notes in a bar instead of two.

9. The following is the boasted melody of the nevertheless exquisite poet of the *Rape of the Lock,*—exquisite in his wit and fancy, though not in his numbers. The reader will observe that it is literally *see-saw.*

10. It might, indeed, be objected to the verse of Milton, that it exhibits too constant a perfection of this kind [variety in phrase and accent]. It sometimes forces upon us too great a sense of consciousness on the part of the composer. We miss the first sprightly runnings of verse,—the ease and sweetness of spontaneity. Milton, I think, also too often condenses weight into heaviness.

11. The mastery of rime consists in never writing it for its own sake, or at least never appearing to do so; in knowing how to vary it, to give it novelty, to render it more or less strong, to divide it (when not in couplets) at the proper intervals, to repeat it many times where luxury or animal spirits demand it, to impress an affecting or startling remark with it, and to make it, in comic poetry, a new and surprising addition to the jest.

family, in the belief that they have been opening his
letters. But all of these unfriendly and random comments are balanced by others in quite different vein.[41]
More than this, the difficulties came, in point of time,
after the period of initial influence—after the tendencies had been established so firmly that only the realization of his maturing abilities led Keats to strike out
independently, not like one who was to write his name
in water, but with the confidence of one who was to be
among the English poets after his death. And as evidence that his own point of view was quite similar to
that of Hunt we may note briefly certain of Keats's
comments on poetry, and on the sonnet in particular.

9

Although Keats never wrote, as did Hunt, an essay
showing his conception of the sonnet, nor gave or-
ganized expression to his theory of poetry, it is reasonably simple to indicate both. For there is, scattered
through the letters and poems, a fairly consistent body
of opinion, a large part of which has to do with the
sonnet form; and it is significantly like that of Hunt.
One may argue that since Hunt's theory was written
after the death of Keats, and since he so freely ac-
knowledged the younger poet's genius, the influence
may rather have been from Keats to Hunt. There is
something to be said for this point of view. Barnette
Miller, for example, finds that by 1820 the influence of
Hunt is reduced to minor considerations, and that by
1831, in "The Gentle Armour," Hunt is the imitator
of Keats.[42] But there still remains the evidence quoted
above to show that Hunt's later opinion was simply
the outgrowth of his earlier attitude, and this we know
to have been the important factor in the formulation

of Keats's thought, even though the possibility of mutual influence be recognized.

With that self-criticism which is in no small part the stuff of genius, Keats consistently disparages his own poetic accomplishment. There was never any danger that he would succumb, as he felt Hunt had, to the delusion of thinking himself a great poet. That rare moment when he felt that he might be among the English poets after his death was too frequently countered by the self-inflicted despair that comes only to those who vision a goal beyond human attainment, yet who can be satisfied with nothing less than a lifelong struggle towards its achievement. And the sonnet form particularly challenged him with its demand for discipline, restraint, and conformity to established patterns.

So he is half apologetic as he writes in the preface to the 1817 volume: "The short pieces in the middle of the book, as well as some of the sonnets, were written at an earlier period than the rest of the poems." And he protests to Charles Cowden Clarke that he prefers Hunt's treatment of the grasshopper-and-cricket theme (written in friendly competition) to his own.[43] Again, in the "Epistle to My Brother George," he writes:

> As to my sonnets, though none else should heed them,
> I feel delighted, still, that you should read them.*

And two years later, in a letter to George in America, he writes that "Brown has been here rummaging up some of my old sins—that is to say sonnets."[44]

There can be little question that the difficulties Keats felt to be inherent in the sonnet form were the

---

*Lines 118-19. Yet his best poetry to that date (1817) had been the sonnets. In connection with the epistle and the problem of influence it is not often noted that "in lower style, and almost/ forgotten, are the series of seven letters in verse (uneasy anapests [tetrameters]) scribbled off by Hunt in hit-or-miss fashion that year [1816]." [Blunden, *op. cit.*, pp. 62-63.]

result of a discipline far more severe than any he had
experienced in writing relatively lax couplets under
Hunt's influence. If, as seems likely, this looseness of
heroic couplet texture was an attempt to substitute
naturalness for the artificiality of the eighteenth century, it was soon carried to an extreme by Hunt, and,
following him, by Keats. But sonnet structure is not
consistent with laxness—although stiffness is not the
necessary alternative—and Keats, in his comments on
the form, seems bothered by his inability to distinguish
clearly between freedom and license. Yet it is, finally,
in his disciplined freedom that Keats is most modern.*

If, however, Keats becomes overlax at times in seek-
ing freedom, it is the result not of ignorance, but of
carrying too far a well-defined poetic "axiom" (as he
calls it) that "if poetry come not as naturally as the
leaves to a tree, it had better not come at all."[45] It is
for this naturalness that he acclaims the sonnets of
Shakespeare when he writes, "they seem so full of fine
things said unintentionally—in the intensity of working out conceits."[46] And it is as a result of his desire
for naturalness that he attempts the experimental
sonnet, "If by dull rhymes . . . " and writes, "I have
been endeavoring to discover a better sonnet stanza
than we have. The legitimate does not suit the language over well from the pouncing rhymes. . . . "[47]
The form is obviously disturbing him, forcing him
into expression that is unnatural. Again he writes,
"What imagination I have I shall enjoy, and greatly,
for I have experienced the satisfaction of having great
conceptions without the trouble of sonneteering"[48]—
great conceptions, we may assume, that cannot "sur-

---

*With regard to modern trends in sonnet structure, Lewis G. Sterner [*The
Sonnet in America*] quotes answers from Babette Deutsch, Clement Wood,
and W. R. Benét, among others, to an inquiry. They find, and approve, a more
flexible cadence and approximate rime. In both respects Keats is strikingly
modern.

prise by a fine excess" when they must be molded into shape by "tagging some rhymes."[49]

A corollary to the desire for naturalness is found in Keats's belief that poetry should come as the result of personal emotion, not of writing for its own sake. In this he is not fully consistent, as the poems written in competition with Hunt and others indicate; but he would doubtless consider these mere exercises, not poetry. He refused to write a serious eulogistic sonnet on Spenser at the request of Reynolds' sister, Mrs. Longmore, because he could not command the mood;[50] and his objection to the "Lines on Seeing a Lock of Milton's Hair" was that "I did [it] at Hunt's at his request—perhaps I should have done something better alone and at home."[51] On the walking tour of Scotland he wrote a sonnet in Burns's cottage "for the mere sake of writing some lines under the roof," but they were so unsatisfactory that he would not transcribe them in his letter.[52] And again, after trying to record his response to Dante's episode of Paolo and Francesca, he was forced to conclude that "there are fourteen lines, but nothing of what I felt in it."[53] It was about this time that he reached the decision which indicates his real poetic feeling:

I have come to this resolution—never to write for the sake of writing or making a poem, but from running over with any little knowledge or experience which many years of reflection may perhaps give me; otherwise I will be dumb.*

It was this integrity of purpose that Hunt admired most in the poetry of Keats. Hunt answered Reynolds' complaint that the poetry of many of his contemporaries contained too much of the personal element, with the statement that "it is to Mr. Keats's poetry

---

*Letter 107. Note that the statement is almost a paraphrase of Wordsworth's definition of poetry as the "spontaneous overflow of powerful feelings: it takes its origin from emotion recollected in tranquility."

what particular companionship is to solitude, both excellent things, when genuine; and we are mistaken if he himself does not partake more of both than his intelligent critic supposes."[54] Again, his review of the 1817 volume praises Keats for avoiding imitation of the French and other models, and says of the newcomer's poems:

... the work is not one of mere imitation, or a compilation of ingenious and promising things that merely announce better, and that after all might only help to keep up a bad system; but here is a young poet giving himself up to his own impressions, and revelling in real poetry for its own sake.[55]

And he closes his "Essay on the ... Sonnet" with a plea for poets to write the thing close to themselves—to give expression to the personal emotion.

Hunt and Keats are at one not only in these matters of general theory, but also (although neither poet was entirely consistent in his application of theory to practice) in many of the specific points each makes. The following comparative statements will indicate this relationship:

Hunt	*Keats*
[The sonnet] must confine itself to one leading idea, thought, or feeling. ["Essay"]	[In the rondeau-like "Bards of Passion"] you have one idea amplified with greater ease and more delight and freedom than in the sonnet. [Letter 93]
[It must] leave in the reader's mind no sense of irrelevancy or insufficiency. ["Essay"] [Of "Grecian Urn," st. 2] ... an intensity of the sentiment, at once original in the idea, and going home, like an old thought, to the heart. ["Mr.	The last [line of a sonnet by Reynolds] has "tender and true." We must cut this, and not be rattlesnaked into any more of the like. [Letter 41] Poetry should surprise by a fine excess, and not by singularity; it should strike the reader as a

Hunt	Keats
Keats," in *Lord Byron and . . . Contemporaries*]	wording of his own highest thoughts, and appear almost a remembrance. Its touches of beauty should never be half-way, thereby making the reader breathless instead of content. [Letter 48]
It must not have a speck of obscurity. ["Essay"]	Here are the poems; they will explain themselves, as all poems should do without comment. [Letter 93]
It must not have a superfluous word. ["Essay"]	My feelings entirely fall in with yours [Haydon] in regard to the ellipsis.* [Letter 6]
Its music, throughout, must be as varied as it is suitable; more or less strong, or sweet, according to the subject; but never weak or monotonous, unless monotony itself be the effect desired. ["Essay"] Mark [in stanza describing Archimago's hermitage *(F. Q. I.* 34)] . . . the intonation of the vowels. [*Imagination and Fancy,* p. 71]	One of Keats's favorite topics of conversation [writes Bailey] was the principle of melody in verse, which he believed to consist in the adroit management of open and close vowels. He had a theory that vowels could be as skillfully combined and interchanged as differing notes of music, and that all sense of monotony was to be avoided, except when expressive of a special purpose.†[56]
The close must be equally impressive and unaffected; not epigrammatic . . . but simple, conclusive, and satisfactory; strength being paramount, where such elevation is natural, otherwise on a level with sere-	The rise, the progress, the setting of imagery should, like the sun, come natural to him [the reader], shine over him, and set soberly, although in magnificance, leaving him in the luxury of twilight. [Letter 48]

---

*Verse 13 of sonnet 21 was shortened to avoid forced rime and wordiness.
† Hunt also sided with Keats against Wordsworth that Shakespeare's line, "The singing masons building roofs of gold," was desirably onomatopoetic [Hunt, *Lord Byron and . . . Contemporaries,* vol. I, pp. 430-31].

Hunt	Keats
nity; flowing in calmness, or grand in manifestation of power withheld. ["Essay"]	Up to its climax and then dying proudly. ["Epistle to Clarke," line 61] The other [Shakespearean sonnet] ... appears too elegiac— and the couplet at the end of it has seldom a pleasing effect. [Letter 114]
[Milton's verse] sometimes forces upon us too great a sense of consciousness on the part of the composer. ["What is Poetry"]	Miltonic verse cannot be written but in an artful, or, rather, artist's humour. . . . Miltonic verse cannot be written, but is the verse of art. I wish to devote myself to another sensation. [Letter 147]
The following is the boasted melody of the ... *Rape of the Lock*. ... The reader will observe that it is literally see-saw. ["What is Poetry"]	... with a puling infant's force They sway'd about upon a rocking horse, And thought it Pegasus ... were closely wed To musty laws lined out with wretched rule And compass vile. . . . ["Sleep and Poetry," ll. 185-87; 194-96]
The mastery of rime consists in never writing it for its own sake, or at least never appearing to do so. ["What is Poetry"]	And while, for rhymes, I search around the poles. ["To My Brothers," l. 5] If by dull rhymes our English must be chain'd. ["On the Sonnet," l. 1; and *cf*. entire sonnet]

Certain of the foregoing items may justifiably be ascribed to the natural inclination of all poets to arrive at conclusions about their art, and hence may have been reached independently by both Hunt and Keats. But in the light of their close association and the large

number of parallels here presented the only reasonable
conclusion to be drawn is that in large part either
Keats's poetic theory owes an important debt to the
older writer, or that many of their corresponding ideas
were derived mutually from their critical discussions
and poetic exercises. Hunt was always conscious of
technique in discussing poetry; he himself declared
that at the time of writing "Endymion" Keats had not
yet "settled with himself any principle of versification,"[57] so surely he would not have hesitated to
criticise his friend during the period of literary association. That he did not neglect craftsmanship in
writing about the work of Keats has already been
demonstrated, and his commentary on "The Eve of
Saint Agnes" is practically a summary of the points
made in the theory outlined above. He writes:

> Let the student of poetry observe, that in all the luxury of *The
> Eve of Saint Agnes* there is nothing of the conventional craft of
> artificial writers; no heaping up of words or similes for their own
> sakes or the rhyme's sake; no gaudy commonplaces; no borrowed
> airs of earnestness; no tricks of inversion; no substitution of read-
> ing or of ingenious thoughts for feeling and spontaneity; no
> irrelevancy or unfitness of any sort. All flows out of sincerity and
> passion.[58]

10

We know from Keats's own statements and from
his experimental sonnets that he grew restive under
the restrictions of the form, but serious objection must
be raised to the suggestion that he "abandoned" it.
Professor Garrod has attempted to show that the
development of the ode stanza came as an outgrowth
of the poet's dissatisfaction with the existing rime
schemes of the sonnet—the ode being, in effect, a com-
bination of the opening quatrain of the Shakespearean
form and the sestet of the Italian pattern. Thus, rea-

sons Professor Garrod, having hit upon a stanza which contained the best features of the two sonnet forms, Keats wrote only one or two sonnets after April, 1819.[59] But Nelson Bushnell has shown[60] that the experimental sonnet, in which Keats was admittedly trying to break away, was entirely unlike the ode stanza; that the "Ode to Psyche," on which Garrod based much of his argument, does not avoid the "too elegiac" quality objected to by Keats; that the subjects, treatment, and spirit of the odes are complete departures from the sonnets; that the "Lines on . . . Milton's Hair," written a year and a half before the sonnet experiments, has a close approximation to the ode stanza; and that this stanza had been used several times in earlier English poetry. He holds that the sonnet was rejected because it was not suited to the new subjects Keats wished to treat, and hence there was a return to the ode form which he and others had used previously. Both Garrod and Bushnell thus admit that Keats did turn from the form, and Ridley, following Garrod, writes, "It looks as though from this time on [April, 1819, when the "Ode to Psyche" was written] Keats abandoned the sonnet as incorrigible."[61]

It may well be asked, however, whether these statements, so easily picked up and disseminated, are entirely satisfactory as explaining Keats's relationship to the form he used so widely. All poets are faced with exasperating moments in which it seems that the technical demands of their art are insurmountable; and most who, like Keats, are interested in the historical development of poetry and in the variations to be found in its patterns must at times give way to an impulse to try innovations. Too much, therefore, should not be made of the "experimental" sonnet, the unrimed sonnet, nor of those altered rime schemes in which Keats is merely availing himself of a privilege which has been exercised freely by creative artists. More than this, however, it may be asked if Keats did really abandon the sonnet form. The evidence on which the assertion is usually made has to do with the assumption that after April, 1819, there are only three extant sonnets written by the poet. But for how long after April, 1819? Actually for only eight months, since he had practically given up writing by December of that year, the remaining fourteen months of life being laid in pawn to death. And dating of the sonnets must, even with the care of Finney's approach, remain relatively tentative. Let us, however, allow only these three and ask what else was occupying Keats's time during these eight months. Personally, he was torn by a hopeless love for Fanny Brawne, by lack of funds, and by a rapidly developing mortal illness. Poetically, he was finally attempting the form which he had long desired—the drama; he wrote "Otho the Great," the fragment of "King Stephen," and the "Gripus" fragment. He also wrote "Lamia," and was striving for the epic grasp in "The Fall of Hyperion." And he wrote the great odes. It would be thoroughly reasonable to assume that the poet's mind was occupied with problems, themes, and forms quite different from those normally associated with the sonnet, and that there might be little time or spirit for more than the three allowed him. He wrote none (by Finney's dating) during the composition of "Endymion." But another point should be emphasized. Conditionally granting with Bushnell that the subjects, treatment, and spirit of the odes are complete departures (which is too strong) from the sonnets, the fact remains that they do present basically emotional themes, and single leading ideas, in relatively brief space as contrasted with the drama, narrative, or epic. They would serve, therefore, as an outlet for the emotional expression that might otherwise have been treated in the sonnet, and they came as an interesting new medium which might reasonably replace for a time the vexing sonnet form.

It should, then, be said that for a brief time Keats replaced his emphasis on the sonnet by a corresponding emphasis on the ode, rather than that he "abandoned the sonnet as incorrigible." And evidence to warrant the assumption that he would, in time, have re-emphasized the earlier form—and that it would have been greatly perfected as a result of his mastery of the ode—is found in the fact that he "abandoned" "Hyperion" because "Miltonic verse cannot be written, but is the verse of art." The phrase is almost an exact analysis of his dissatisfaction with the sonnet form. Yet he returned to the poem in "The Fall of Hyperion" with a new vision and accomplishment.*

Conclusion

We may now summarize briefly the extent of Keats's knowledge and theory concerning the sonnet. While he did not offer any definition of the term, we have seen that in the main his conception of its nature was that held by Leigh Hunt. He did not limit his use to the Italian model, however, as Hunt might have wished, but admitted the Shakespearean form as well, incorporating into it those non-Elizabethan qualities that have made it, since Keats's day, a more flexible and worthier companion to the traditional Petrarchan type.

Keats's knowledge of the Italian sonnet may have come from several sources. Havens is in error, however, when he writes, "As he rarely disregarded the

---

*Note that Wordsworth "abandoned" the sonnet during 1804-05, but wrote twenty in 1806, and an average of ten each year until 1817. He then "abandoned" it again during 1817-18, but wrote nearly two hundred during 1819-21 [Havens, op. cit., p. 531].

pauses and turn, and as he was interested in Italian poetry, he may have derived his rime schemes, and in part his conception of the sonnet, from Petrarch, Dante, and their countrymen."[62] It is as late as April 27, 1818, that Keats informs Reynolds, "I . . . shall learn Greek, and very likely Italian,"[63] indicating that as yet no active interest in the language had been aroused. Then followed the four months of the walking tour; and it is not until September, 1819, that he is able to write to Taylor, "Am now occupied . . . studying Italian,"[64] and to his brother in America, "In the course of a few months I shall be as good an Italian scholar as I am a French one. I am reading Ariosto at present, not managing more than six or eight stanzas at a time. . . . I shall never become attached to a foreign idiom, so as to put it into my writings."[65] Further, Keats had turned from the Petrarchan to the Shakespearean form by the beginning of 1818.

But if he did not go directly to the Italian models, Hunt did, and was translating sonnets from Filicaia in 1816, and publishing translations of Castiglioni's quatorzains (on which he had undoubtedly been working earlier) in 1823.[66] Keats's early admiration for Milton and Wordsworth would further increase his interest in the Petrarchan model, but Professor Garrod is clearly in error when he holds that the Italian influence should be ascribed to them rather than to Hunt.[67] We have already seen, and shall present corroborating evidence below, that the influence of Milton and Wordsworth must be considered secondary to that of Keats's friend. On the other hand, Havens goes too far in an opposite direction when he states:

How it is that they [Keats's sonnets] were uninfluenced by the sonnets of Wordsworth, whom their author deeply admired, and of Milton, whose *Paradise Lost* transformed his other poetry, it is

hard to say, unless the Della Cruscan-Italian-Elizabethan conceptions of the sonnet possessed him so completely that he did not
admire, or, as is more probable, was disinclined to write, Miltonic
sonnets.[68]

This comes very close to mere quibbling. Is it not
more reasonable, in the light of the foregoing sections
of our study, to suggest that the general influence,
which cannot be denied, of both Milton and Wordsworth was overshadowed by the more immediate influence of Hunt, whose poetic theory has been shown
to parallel that of Keats? It was not that he followed
Milton and Wordsworth less, but that he followed
Hunt more.*

However complex his source, he knew and used the
form. He must also, as an artist, have understood
something of the characteristic beauties inherent in the
pattern; and while the sonnets do not have the melodic
perfection of the odes, it should be remembered that
they represent in large part the apprenticeship during
which the poet was learning his craft—just as the odes
in their turn stand as the masterpiece that placed him
"among the English poets" after a death that denied
this craftsman his season of labor.

It is strange that Keats never mentions the sonnets
of Spenser, and that he never quotes from them, but
there is no reason to believe, in the light of his admiration for the Elizabethan, that he was unacquainted
with them. The reason for the omission is probably
twofold. First, the Spenserian was not an important
nor popular sonnet form during the century preceding
Keats, and when the Italian pattern was not used the
almost universal choice was the Shakespearean. And
second, Hunt once more seems to have exerted an in-

---

*Note that the spirit for which Keats [letter 50] praises Wordsworth's sonnet
is exactly that which we call Miltonic: "When I think of Wordsworth's sonnet
'Vanguard of Liberty! ye men of Kent!' the degenerate race about me are
pulvis ipecac. simplex—a strong dose."

fluence, for his clearly defined objections to the Spenserian form would probably be sufficient to deter his youthful admirer from attempting it.

Hunt, having used the Shakespearean pattern in his *Juvenilia,* was more lenient with regard to it, limiting his opinion to the statement that it was "unartistical"[69] except in the hands of Shakespeare himself. But even here his attitude may have served as a retarding influence on Keats, until such time, early in 1818, as the younger poet was no longer willing to follow slavishly the dicta of others; and by that time he had discovered, at the source, the full strength of Shakespeare's sonnets.

If there was any firsthand influence of eighteenth-century writings it was slight, for all that the period had to offer was contained with more telling effect in the works of its principal forerunner, Milton, and its principal successor, Wordsworth. The first stood as a model for pre-Romantic opposition to the stiffness of pseudo-classicism; the second carried to fulfillment the disorganized attempts of the Milton imitators, giving to the sonnet an integrity of structure and spirit that had been missing for a century and a half.

But in none of these earlier writers could Keats find any body of criticism or legislation regarding the sonnet form. It was possible for him to determine the general characteristics from his reading and study, but there would be little to suggest standards, and the models he might have known would offer precedent for an almost limitless variation. Yet his work is unusually regular in its outward form. The answer can only be that since Leigh Hunt had given probably more consideration to the sonnet as a form than had any previous writer, and that since Keats became his friend during the most active months both of Hunt's critical life and Keats's metamorphosis from surgeon to poet, we must look to Hunt as the major influence on Keats's sonnets. To do so is to find an impressive agreement between the theories of the two writers, and an early emulation by Keats that was in time to be replaced by the independent judgment of his later period.

Part Two:

The Sonnets of John Keats:
A Critical and Comparative Study

Let us inspect the Lyre, and weigh the stress
Of every chord, and see what may be gain'd
By ear industrious, and attention meet . . .

["On the Sonnet"]

A NOTE ON THE METHOD EMPLOYED IN THIS SECTION

One can scarcely hope that all readers will be in agreement as to position or degree of each accent used in a study such as this; yet it should be possible to assign to the verses a reading that will be at once natural and consistent, and that may be allowed for purposes of comparison and determination of conclusions.

In the present approach, the normal accentuation of words has been given preference, as has a natural development of thought and phrasing, thus avoiding an artificial or "singsong" reading of the lines. In every respect a consistent analysis of the sonnets of all writers considered has been made.

In oral reading of the sonnets, shades of emphasis will normally be indicated by means of the half accent. For purposes of computing metrical variations, however, these compromise accents must be converted into accented (/) or unaccented (x) symbols for sharper definition of effects. This has been done in the present study.

The blending of sounds in verse may be so subtle as practically to defy analysis. Two considerations have, therefore, been permitted to govern this aspect of the study: (1) emphasis and (2) position of the vowels or consonants involved.

Other details of method will be clear from comments in text or notes.

THE SONNETS OF JOHN KEATS: A CRITICAL AND COMPARATIVE STUDY

In his article on Keats in *Imagination and Fancy*, Hunt, in a statement that may well open the present section of our study, writes, "He died at five-and-twenty; he had not revised his earlier works, nor given his genius its last pruning."[1] The commentary is especially applicable to the sonnets, where so frequently revision did not follow the poet's dissatisfaction. Many of them, moreover, remained unpublished, apparently untouched after once being set down, and many were on subjects of momentary interest only. It might seem grossly unfair, from this point of view, to characterize a poet's versecraft on the basis of such work as might never, except for his early death, have become known. But it is, after all, in these "unpruned" examples that we find the elements out of which the poet builds—that we come, in many respects, nearer to the craftsman at work—and a cross section of the total product, finished and unfinished, should be particularly revealing.

A threefold advantage accrues to the objective and comparative method employed in the following pages. Keats's relationship to the writers in whom he expressed greatest interest (Spenser, Shakespeare, Milton, Wordsworth, and Hunt [with Bowles admitted as an eighteenth-century balance]) can be established. In doing so, incidental characteristics of the other poets' versecraft will be revealed. And finally, the comparative approach, in spanning two and a half centuries of work by the leading sonneteers, offers a glimpse of technical changes that have taken place in English treatment of the form.

I. Form and Content

An approach from the general to the particular is desirable in any verse analysis, since in this way a necessary orientation is established in anticipation of the more subtle phases of discussion. With the reader, the idea will normally take precedence over form; with the poet, the two elements are likely to be arrived at concurrently; but with the student of versecraft, whose interest is for the moment centered on the sonnet as a literary type, the point of departure may well be basic patterns. We shall therefore determine first Keats's use of form, and secondly the manner in which his themes are made a part of structure.

1

A summarized tabulation of representative octave and sestet rime schemes for the Petrarchan sonnet has already been given (p. 20 and Tables I and II). It is clear from these tables that insistence on rigid conformity to an invariable octave, or on a minimum variation in the sestet, has been on authority other than that of historical sonnet development, and is an artificial standard advanced by modern purists. On the other hand, the true artist will not resort to mere laxness because the form in which he writes is rigid. Reference to the tables will indicate that Keats never evades the issue so far as the octave is concerned, though ample precedent existed,* and that his use of the sestet is likewise quite in conformity with such principles of structure as he might have known. Indeed, when using either the Petrarchan or Shakespearean form Keats is consistently regular. When he turns from the established patterns he is quite obvious-

---

*Note, however, that of the twenty-eight Italian sonnets written early enough to have influenced Keats, Hunt has only one that does not conform to the *abbaabba* pattern. Clearly he favored the invariable octave.

ly experimenting (the privilege of all writers), and attempting to make a desirable contribution to English prosody—not side-stepping the responsibilities demanded by the accepted patterns.

Of sixty-six* sonnets, Keats wrote, by types, forty-five Petrarchan, fifteen Shakespearean, and six irregular. His failure to use the Spenserian form, which he must have known, has already been mentioned, and since the Shakespearean was not used by him until after the influence of Hunt had started to wane (though Keats's intensive study of Shakespeare also came about the same time), we may conclude that Hunt's attitude determined to a large degree the early choice made by Keats. It will be observed from Table IV that approximately forty sonnets were written before Keats turned to the non-Petrarchan types, and that only one experimental in form was written during the early period.

TABLE IV
DISTRIBUTION OF RIME SCHEMES IN KEATS'S SONNETS

Pattern		Occurrences	Sonnet Numbers
			Petrarchan
abbaabba	cdcdcd	24	2, 3, 4, 7, 9, 10, 11, 12, 13, 16, 17, 18, 19, 20, 21 [cdcd()d], 24, 31, 33, 35, 36, 38, 40, 44, 52.
”	cdecde	6	6, 14, 22, 23, 29, 32.
”	cdedec	4	26, 37, 39, 51.
”	cdcdee	3	15, 41, 54.
”	cddcdc	2	5, 8.
”	cddcee	2	27, 34.
”	cdccdd	1	64.
”	cdcddc	1	28.
”	cdcede	1	30.
”	cdedce	1	25.
			Shakespearean
abab cdcd efef	gg	15	42, 43, 45, 46, 48, 49, 50, 53, 55, 57, 58, 59, 61, 65, 66.
			Irregular
abab cdcd ddedee		1	1
Unrimed, assonating		1	47
abab cbcb dede [] []		1	56
abab cdcd bcefef		1	60
abab cdcd efeggf		1	62
abcabdcabcdede		1	63

*The light, occasional sonnet "To A. G. S." was published too late to be included in the present study. It is in the Shakespearean pattern, quite typical of Keats's light-verse technique, and would in no way alter the conclusions here offered, except to modify the number of Shakespearean sonnets to 16, and the total sonnets to 67.

Several important points should be noted in connection with Table IV. First is the invariable octave, to which reference has already been made, in the Petrarchan form. Despite the example of Wordsworth, Keats never alters the rigid *abbaabba* scheme, and, except for occasions when his failure to hit readily upon a rime word seems to cause a change in direction of thought, manages it very well. That he realized his lack of facility in discovering appropriate rimes is suggested in two sonnets. In number 20 he writes:

> And while, for rhymes, I search around the poles;

and in the experimental sonnet, number 63—in commenting on which he objects to the "pouncing rhymes" and couplets found in the accepted forms— he writes in similar vein:

> If by dull rhymes our English must be chain'd . . .
> Let us find out, if we must be constrain'd,
> Sandals more interwoven and complete
> To fit the naked foot of Poesy . . .

Yet, considering the age in which he lived, Keats has relatively few of the inversions that commonly result from rime difficulty. Instead, he frequently selects an inferior or obvious word (a point made by Wilson in his *Quarterly Review* attack on "Endymion"), or permits an unnecessary repetition to bridge the gap caused by an unfortunate rime choice, as in the following lines from sonnet number 55, where the word "wist" and the phrase "even such" seem concessions to the rime:

> Read me a lesson, Muse, and speak it loud
> Upon the top of Nevis, blind in mist!
> I look into the chasms, and a shroud
> Vaporous doth hide them,—just so much I wist
> Mankind do know of hell; I look o'erhead,

And there is sullen mist,—even so much
Mankind can tell of heaven; mist is spread
Before the earth, beneath me,—even such,
Even so vague is man's sight of himself! . . .

Another point of interest regarding Table IV is the prevalence of the *cdcdcd* sestet. In this, as is natural, Keats seems to feel most sure of himself, and he uses it as the form for the opening sonnet (and poem) in the 1817 volume—the dedicatory sonnet to Leigh Hunt. There is probably no more satisfactory pattern for the Italian sestet, although *cdecde* (his second choice) has similar features. In the first place, the alternating arrangement is fairly easy to write; and in the second place, it has an excellent effect on the reader. It has the two-rime unity of the octave without the closely knit bracing and overlapping of the octave pattern. Thus, after eight verses in which the way must be carefully followed, the reader moves steadily forward, in easy strides, to a satisfying conclusion. Likewise the poet, after synthesizing his thought with the extreme care demanded by the brace rimes, finds himself in a section where he can develop his ideas adequately and with a minimum concession to the rime words. Both for artistic unity and satisfactory development of thought, therefore, Keats uses what is probably the most desirable of the many possible Italian patterns, and his second and third choices are only slightly less unified, in that they are built on three rime sounds.

There was little if any precedent for change in the Shakespearean form, and for the most part Keats holds faithfully to the rime scheme. Yet three of the six experimental sonnets open with the *abab cdcd* of the Shakespearean quatrains, and a fourth (the unfinished Ronsard translation) with only a slight variation, *abab cbcb;* and in each instance but the latter the sonnets close with what is practically a Petrarchan sestet. This might have been assumed, from the foregoing discussion, to be the move Keats would make in altering the sonnet form. He favored the sestet of the Italian pattern, and he disliked the closing couplet of the Shakespearean (though the early experiment, number 1, ends with a couplet). The opening quatrains of the Shakespearean sonnet should, therefore, combine appropriately with the sestet of the Petrarchan to give a satisfactory new arrangement. Whether or not Keats followed this line of reasoning, his experiments in four of six cases (practically all, since one of the others is unrimed) resulted in a blending of this kind. But it was not successful. The average reader, on the assumption of regularity of recurrence in poetry, prefers the patterns that are most familiar to him; and none is more familiar than the quatrain with alternating rime. When therefore, as in the following, number 62, he is led through two normal quatrains, and three verses of a third, his natural anticipation is that the satisfying rime will appear in the expected position. Instead, Keats introduces a couplet and delays the balancing rime until the last verse. Great skill would be required to control the phrasing and cadences in such a way that this violation would possess an artistic justification, and this Keats seems not to have had at the moment of writing:

How fever'd is the man, who cannot look	a
Upon his mortal days with temperate blood,	b
Who vexes all the leaves of his life's book,	a
And robs his fair name of its maidenhood;	b
It is as if the rose should pluck herself,	c
Or the ripe plum finger its misty bloom,	d
As if a naiad, like a meddling elf,	c
Should darken her pure grot with muddy gloom;	d
But the rose leaves herself upon the briar,	e
For winds to kiss and grateful bees to feed,	f

And the ripe plum still wears its dim attire,   e
The undisturbed lake has crystal space;   g
Why then should man, teasing the world for grace,   g
Spoil his salvation for a fierce miscreed?   f

The sonnet just read may be advantageously compared with the following, number 60, in which a similar type of variation occurs:

O soft embalmer of the still midnight,   a
Shutting, with careful fingers and benign,   b
Our gloom-pleas'd eyes, embower'd from the light,   a
Enshaded in forgetfulness divine: b
O soothest Sleep! if so it please thee, close   c
In midst of this thine hymn my willing eyes,   d
Or wait the "amen" ere thy poppy throws   c
Around my bed its lulling charities.   d
Then save me, or the passed day will shine   b
Upon my pillow, breeding many woes,—   c
Save me from curious conscience, that still lords e
Its strength for darkness, burrowing like a mole; f
Turn the key deftly in the oiled wards,   e
And seal the hushed casket of my soul.   f

Here the result is far more successful, and for two reasons. First, what would be the third quatrain is not carried into its third verse, only two lines being affected, and a complete quatrain is left for the close of the sonnet. But more important is the concession (which prevents stumbling on these verses) made to the reader's ear. Observe that the first quatrain not only rimes alternately but also assonates in all rime words (mid*n*ight—ben*i*gn—l*i*ght—div*i*ne). The second quatrain also rimes alternately, carries the voiced *s* through the rime words (close—eyes—throw*s*—charitie*s*), and ends on an approximate rime *(charities)* which qualifies the sound resolution. Then what would be the third quatrain begins, but its first rime sound *(shine)* is definitely established in the reader's mind from the opening quatrain, and its second *(woes)*, with its voiced *s*, is both an echo of, and in rime with, parts of the second quatrain. This serves to absorb the abrupt change and the reader accepts *lords* tentatively. He is then given a strong assonance between w*o*es and m*o*le, which leads him over into the closing two lines with a blended effect that is quite agreeable.*

The unrimed sonnet, number 47, in which assonance again plays an important role, is an interesting venture, and the skill with which the repetitions and sound devices are controlled makes one scarcely conscious of the absence of rime. The other experiment, number 63, in which the poet was consciously trying to establish a new rime scheme, has been adequately characterized by Keats himself: "I have been endeavouring to discover a better sonnet stanza than we have. The legitimate does not suit the language over well from the pouncing rimes—the other kind appears too elegiac —and the couplet at the end of it has seldom a pleasing effect—I do not pretend to have succeeded."[2] His failure was the result not so much of rime scheme as of unfortunate use, in key positions, of rimes approximate either in sound or accent. A reader coming to an unfamiliar stanza naturally follows through it tentatively, trying to catch the pattern. Unless the rimes are exact and sharply defined (or skillfully modulated as in the preceding example) he will be thrown off the familiar track, and the stanza will lose such unity as it might otherwise have.

Generally speaking, then, we may conclude that Keats was reasonably conservative in his use of the sonnet form. In an age when the quatorzain was being revived and extensively written, and when struc-

---

*Was Keats conscious of these details? Possibly not; the creative artist masters his tools; he makes them a part of his subconscious equipment. But there can be no question that Keats, or any serious poet, could analyze his effects as we have done. *Cf.* Bailey's comments on Keats's theory of the musical value of vowels, above, p. 63.

tural experimentation was the rule in lyrical composition, more than 80 per cent of his sonnets are in forms both artistically and legislatively acceptable. Of the others, there are the six admittedly experimental (less than 10 per cent of the whole), and to these may be added, by those who object to the independent closing couplet in the Italian sonnet, six that employ the device. Concerning the latter we need say only that in these instances the poet's ear seems not to have found sufficient dissatisfaction to cause revision. As employment of the couplet was amply warranted by precedent, Keats would have no reason to hesitate in its use if the thought development seemed adapted to it.

2

The principal contribution of Milton and the eighteenth-century poets to sonnet development was, as we have seen, an extension of the range of subject matter, forcing love from its dominant Elizabethan position into one commensurate with other themes. And while an examination of the details of imagery and thought in sixteenth-century quatorzains shows a wide range of interests drawn upon for illustrative material, these occupied a position of importance secondary to that of love. With the precedent set by Milton, Bowles, and Wordsworth, however, Keats could feel free to employ the quatorzain for any subject that he felt merited attention* (see Table V).

An interesting sidelight on Keats's interpretation of the creative process is found in Tables IV and V. It

*Including, by both Keats and Hunt, the use of sonnets for comic effect. A detailed analysis of the quatorzains for references to persons, characters, and places will reveal a rich background. When a specific reference can be called up to illuminate an entire passage, as so frequently happens in Keats, it forms a definite part of the poet's equipment and sets him apart from the immature versifier who must, through weakness, generalize themes and overwrite.

has been noted that a free choice in the matter of subjects has been balanced by a fairly rigid adherence to the standard forms. Keats apparently realized that the "realms of gold" are unlimited, and that any subject may be made the stuff of poetry if its treatment conforms to the higher imaginative expression—if, that is to say, its treatment is poetic. But poetic treat-

TABLE V
PRINCIPAL THEMES IN KEATS'S SONNETS
Theme and Sonnet Numbers

Art: 21, 35, 36, 37.

Brothers: 15, 20.

Cities: 5, 12.

Fame: 3, 18, 25, 42, 52, 61, 62.

Friends: Brawne, 59, 65, 66.
  Haydon, 18, 21, 36, 64.
  Hunt (see Poets)
  Reynolds, 46, 47, 49.
  Wells, 13.
  Wylie, 24.

Friendship: 5, 13, 17, 23, 49.

Genius: 18, 25.

Humanity: 48, 55, 62.

Learning: 27, 47.

Love and Women: 6, 9, 10, 11, 19, 26, 32, 37, 42, 43, 46, 56, 58, 61, 65, 66.

Music: 8, 54.

Nature: General description, 5, 8, 15, 17, 32, 44, 46, 48, 52, 59.
  Its effect on man, 12, 14, 19, 27, 30, 34, 39, 43, 45, 50, 51, 55.
  Insect, bird, animal life, 29, 40, 47.
  Roses, 13.
  Nature worship, 33.

Poems and Plays:
  Floure and Lefe, 34.
  Homer (Chapman's), 16.
  House of Mourning (Scott), 64.
  King Lear, 41.

Poems and Plays (continued):
  Paolo and Francesca (Dante), 58.
  Rimini (Hunt), 38.
  Sonnet (Reynolds), 46.
  Sonnet on Dover (Wordsworth), 64.
  Stranger, The (play), 54.

Poetry: General, 31, 63.
  Its pleasures, 12, 14, 16, 38, 41, 54, 58.
  Its powers, 4, 16, 41.
  His devotion to, 23, 42.
  In nature, 28.

Poets: General, 8, 21, 27, 61.
  Burns, 51, 53.
  Byron, 2.
  Chapman, 16.
  Chatterton, 3.
  Coleridge, 64.
  Homer, 16, 50.
  Hunt, 4, 17, 21, 23, 31, 32, 33.
  Milton, 4, 14, 17.
  Petrarch, 17.
  Sappho, 30.
  Scott, 64.
  Shakespeare, 41.
  Spenser, 4, 45.
  Wordsworth, 21, 64.

Political and National: 1, 4, 14, 18, 22[?], 25, 26, 31.

Religion and Death: 7, 28, 57, 62 [?].

Sleep: 60.

ment implies the discipline and the adherence to standards of organization demanded of the artist in whatever field—standards that, whether or not analyzed as such, have their basis in responses of the human mind. In the historical development of a poetic pattern there will be a gradual adjustment to these standards through trial and error, as has been demonstrated for the sonnet. Artists are free to attempt changes (note the Keats experiments), and such attempts contribute to poetic evolution; but normally the young poet will at first follow the tested patterns until such time as mastery of their principles justifies an independent contribution. Artistically, therefore, Keats seems to have sensed the desirability of holding largely to the traditional sonnet forms, and at the same time to have realized that the themes of poetry are as varied as are the interests of the human heart, and that the tastes and understanding of the poet must be catholic.

But given form and theme, the creative process also implies the appropriate adaptation of one to the other. The most satisfying poem is the one in which neither element intrudes upon the other, but in which both blend to form the unity of impression for which all artists strive. And since we shall be concerned later with the details of phrasing in the sonnets of Keats, only the more general aspects of form-content relationship need be indicated at this point. Our discussion has shown that the quatrain-plus-couplet division of the Shakespearean sonnet invites turns in thought* at one or more of the quatrain divisions; and that in the Italian sonnet, similarly, a natural and desirable turn is suggested by the rime scheme, the break coming at the end of verse eight. Dependent on synthesis of thought, Keats's sonnets may contain no definite turns, or as many as four. Table VI shows that while, like Milton and others, Keats made the form serve the idea instead of forcing the idea into the limits of the form, he did, in general, observe the thought organization suggested by the structural principles of the sonnet as a type. In the majority of cases in the Italian

---

*By a "turn" in thought is meant not merely a changed emphasis, in which similar aspects of an idea are treated supplementally, but rather a balance or antithesis of one attitude with another. Sonnet number 6, with turns in thought following verses four and eight, will illustrate.

form the turn comes at the end of either or both the first quatrain or octave, while in the Shakespearean pattern the turn most frequently occurs at the end of the fourth, eighth, or twelfth verse, corresponding to the quatrain divisions. One point in this connection is of particular interest as bearing upon our earlier discussion of the closing couplet. As we shall see in a later table, there is a definite *pause* at the end of verse

TABLE VI*

TURNS IN THOUGHT IN KEATS'S SONNETS

Italian Form

Verse		Occurrences		Verse		Occurrences
4	(end)	14		11	(middle)	1
5	(middle)	1		11	(end)	3
5	(end)	2		12	(middle)	1
7	(end)	3		12	(end)	3
8	(end)	26		13	(middle)	2
9	(end)	1		13	(end)	1
10	(end)	3		No definite turn		7

Frequency of Turns

Number of turns in sonnet	Sonnet Occurrences
1	19
2	15
3	5

Shakespearean Form

Verse		Occurrences		Verse		Occurrences
3	(end)	1		12	(middle)	2
4	(middle)	1		12	(end)	7
4	(end)	6		13	(end)	1
8	(end)	7		No definite turn		2
10	(end)	3				

Frequency of Turns

Number of turns in sonnet	Sonnet Occurrences
1	12
2	5
3	1
4	1

twelve no less than twenty-seven times in the sonnets of Keats. Yet the combined *turns in thought* at the end of verse twelve number only ten. The conclusion is evident: the presence of a pause at the end of verse twelve does not necessarily imply a following sharply differentiated turn in thought, nor does a couplet rime imply a corresponding thought emphasis. The thought

*The experimental sonnets have been included under the type to which they most closely approximate.

may lead in from the preceding verses with such natural progress that the reader is scarcely conscious of
the closing couplet rimes when they are present, or
in such a way that the independence of the closing
verses is reduced to a minimum.

As to the number of turns in each sonnet, one point
should be observed. It will be noted that of the
sonnets written in the Italian form nineteen have only
one turn, and fifteen have only two. This is approximately the proportion that might be expected from
the nature of the structure, since there are two principal points at either or both of which turns will
normally occur—the end of the first quatrain and the
end of the octave. But one would expect a greater
frequency of turns in the Shakespearean form, since
three relatively independent quatrains naturally suggest the development of thought in three sections,
with the couplet following as a summarizing fourth.
Among the Shakespearean sonnets of Keats, however,
there are twelve with one turn, and only five with
two. Again, the Italian form has proportionately
more occurrences of sonnets with three turns of
thought. The reason for this is probably in part the
lateness of Keats's adoption of the English pattern:
his habits of thought relationship were established in
conformity with the Petrarchan type, and it is natural
that, despite the changed rime scheme, he should trans-
fer these habits, and retain the general bipartite arrangement of material.*

II. MELODY

Stated in general terms, the problem of the poet,
as of any creative artist, is to balance uniformity and
variety—uniformity sufficient to impress the reader

---

*This would tend to support Crosland's theory of bipartite structure. His
error is in insisting dogmatically that all sonnets must conform.

with recurring patterns or effects, that he may thus be made conscious of a satisfying unity of organization; and variety sufficient to prevent the regularity of recurrence from becoming monotonous. We have already observed variety within uniformity as it relates to form and content. We have seen that a pattern is designed for, or results in, unity of impression —its subdivisions balance one another, and its rime scheme emphasizes the recurring units. At the same time, variety is gained by the slight alterations permitted in the rime scheme, by individual synthesis of ideas, and by the use of different patterns (e. g. Italian, Shakespearean, or experimental) within the quatorzain unit.

A device having to do more definitely with impression on the ear—as opposed to the eye and mind appeal of the larger form-content aspects—is melody. It, too, contributes both to unity and variety, since the poet can either repeat similar sounds, or balance them with modified or different sounds. Any complete analysis of melody in a given poem, however, offers almost insurmountable difficulties. There are so many possibilities of shading, blending, and emphasis, and such inequalities in the sensitivity of different readers, that a full treatment would demand consideration of the phonetic value of every consonant and vowel present. This is clearly outside the scope of the present study, but it is possible to indicate here certain of the characteristic melodic devices employed by the poet.

1

Attempts to determine rime correspondence for any but contemporary poets must of necessity be extremely tentative. The spoken language is in a state of such constant flux, and pronunciation differences, even in neighboring sections of an otherwise unified area, are frequently so marked as to prejudice the most cautious statements. This is particularly true for poets of the Elizabethan period and the seventeenth century. The work of Ellis,[3] Jespersen,[4] and others is suggestive, but admittedly cannot be considered final. Because of this relative ignorance, therefore, and its tendency to invalidate conclusions, the aspects of our discussion which are dependent on a knowledge of pronunciation will omit any but incidental consideration of Spenser, Shakespeare, and Milton.*

With the writers of the nineteenth century we are able to proceed, if not with certainty, at least with greater confidence; for there was published in 1791, in London, *A Critical Pronouncing Dictionary and Expositor of the English Language,* by John Walker (1732-1807).† Walker added to his work a lengthy prefatory treatise on the principles of pronunciation and accent, and, in the dictionary itself, recognized such alternative pronunciations as his long philological and lexicographical experience brought to his attention.

In this widely popular volume, then, we have a key to early nineteenth-century orthoëpy written by a

---

*Ellis writes [*On Early English Pronunciation*, Part Three, p. 862]: "[in the sixteenth century] we have entirely left the region of perfect rhymes, and have entered one where occasional rhymes are no guide at all to the pronunciation, and very frequent rhymes are of but slight value."
Of Spenser, Ellis writes [*ibid.*, p. 862]: "Now the extended examination of Spenser's rhymes . . . leads to [the assumption that] his usages cross the known rules of the time . . . so multifariously, that the poet was evidently hampered with the multiplicity of rhyming words . . . and became careless, or satisfied with rough approximations." And of Shakespeare the same author writes [*ibid.*, p. 953]: "Shakespeare, however, did not allow quite so many liberties as Spenser, although his rhymes would be in themselves quite inadequate to determine his pronunciation."
Tentative conclusions will be given in notes for these writers, together with such suggestions as may be based on Ellis' findings. See particularly, in his work, Part Three, pp. 858-996, and Part Four, Chapters IX, X, and XI.

† This volume, "long regarded as the statute book of English Orthoëpy" [*Dictionary of National Biography*, v. 59, p. 75], passed through no fewer than twenty-eight editions between 1791 and 1826. The identification of sounds is naïve, but clear. The present writer has used the third edition (1802) of the work.

contemporary of Wordsworth, Bowles, Hunt, and
Keats. We cannot, of course, ascribe to these writers a
consistency with Walker's norm, but the present section of our study may be made slightly less tentative
because of Walker's book. With the *Dictionary* as our
guide we may analyze the sonnets for their five basic
rime types.

There are, first, the *exact* rimes—those which conform to definition by agreeing exactly in the sound of
the basic emphasized vowel, and in the sound and
accent of such syllables, when present, as follow it;
and differing in the consonants which precede the
vowel. Exact, or normal, rime is the point from which
poets start, and it contributes most fully to the unity
of their rime schemes. Every sonnet of Keats contains
one or more pairs, other types being used (following
precedent) as variants from this norm. The following
examples selected from the first two sonnets will
illustrate the type: *by-die; less-dress; Isle-smile; state-
great-fate.*

These examples, in addition to being exact, are also
single (one-syllable) rimes. Not that all paired words
must be of one syllable, but that the "rime element"
is so satisfied (thus, *band-understand* represents single
rime). But Keats also uses *double rime,* in which the
rime element is dependent on two syllables, as in
tender-defender [9]* ; *being-seeing* [11]; and once he
splits the double rime between two words: *without
her-about her* [61]. In one instance, also, he uses an
approximation to *triple rime,* though not of the exact
type: *defender-Leander* [9].

A second type of rime is that which is *approximate
in sound.* This is distinguished from the first in that
one or more of the elements which would agree pho-
nologically in exact rime will, in this type, be in only

---

* Bracketed numbers refer to sonnets. See Appendix I.

partial agreement, as in the modern pronunciation of *melody-by* and *love-move*. Certain weaknesses in the riming possibilities of the English language make such approximations desirable, and it will be recalled that among poets, if not among purists, there has been recent approval of the type.

Rimes that are approximate in sound fall into two general divisions, depending on whether or not the vowel or consonant is changed; and of the former, distinction may be made between end and medial vowel positions.

In dealing with end-vowels in early nineteenth-century rimes, we are reasonably certain that combinations such as *by-silently* [12] *(or eternities-skies* [52] in plural combinations) would not at that time be forced into an exact relationship. Walker writes:

The unaccented sound of this letter [*y*] at the end of a syllable, like that of *i* in the same situation, is always like the first sound of *e*: thus *vanity, pleurisy,* &c. and if sound alone were consulted might be written *vanitee, pleurisee,* &c.[5]

Indeed, regardless of whether or not pairs of the *by-silently* type were more nearly in agreement in some early period, it seems clear that since the sixteenth century writers have felt no hesitancy in maintaining these combinations as rime acceptable to themselves and most readers. Other typical examples selected from Keats are: *misery-eye* [3]; *try-quietly* [20]; *luxuriously-nigh* [48].

Rimes approximate in medial vowel sound are most difficult to establish, since the writer's pronunciation must be known or conclusions cannot be exact. As the spoken language changes, the rime words of printed poetry remain fixed, and it is frequently impossible to know, with certainty, whether the sounds were approximate or exact when first written. The modern tendency is to establish, as acceptable, pairs of words that have come down in this way, and to admit them as rimes approximate in sound. But in dealing with earlier writers there is always present the possibility that the relationship was once exact, and that one member of the pair has, in the meantime, undergone phonetic change. To the modern reader, for example, the pairing of *join-wine* and *tea-obey* would seem to result in approximate rime; but it is clear that when Alexander Pope employed these combinations they were exact, and that *join* and *tea* have since altered to their present pronunciation. Similarly, Keats's pairing of *Albion-gone* [41] and *ignorance-perchance* [50] were exact, if his pronunciation agreed with that of Walker in the case of *gone (gŏn)* and *ignorance (-ănce)*.

Individual pronunciation habits, if known, would very likely necessitate a change in classification of some of the following pairs, but, as checked against Walker, they are typical of approximate rime as used by Keats and his contemporaries: *fancies-enhances* [9]; *impossible-quell* [45]; *blood-maidenhood* [62]; *gone-tone, breast-waist* [65].

Consonant variations forming approximate rimes result either from substitution of a different consonant, as in *slept-bereft* [58], or from the degree of voicing, as in *rejoice-noise* [20] and *space-haze* [49].

If the different types of rime approximate in sound are accepted tentatively, combined for Keats and the writers with whom he is to be compared,* and a per-

---

*In the comparative tables of Part Two, the same sonnets have been used throughout. They have been chosen from the works almost certainly known by Keats, and the individual selection has been made with two aims: first, to admit those sonnets named by Keats, emphasized by Hunt, or on such themes as, because of Keats's interests, might have appealed to him; and second, to select representative sonnets from the complete range of each poet's work (before 1819 in the case of contemporaries). In this way Keats's characteristics may be seen readily in comparison with those of writers who led in the development of the sonnet form, and the characteristics of that development as a part of English prosodic history may also be observed. The sonnets selected were:

centage figure determined on the basis of the number of sonnets studied, the relationship between Keats, Hunt, Bowles, and Wordsworth (those whose pronunciation can be determined with some degree of certainty) may be indicated. Table VII shows that in this relationship Keats is closer to Hunt than to any of the others in his use of rimes approximate in sound, and that, in the sonnets examined, Wordsworth is comparatively high, and Bowles is correspondingly low. The results of this table should be compared with the next following.

TABLE VII*

COMPARATIVE TABLE INDICATING USE OF RIMES APPROXIMATE IN SOUND

Writer	Sonnet Occurrences	Sonnets Considered	Percentage
Keats	27	65	41
Hunt	10	28	36
Bowles	3	10	30
Wordsworth	9	15	60

A third type of rime is that which is *approximate in accent,* its distinguishing characteristic being that, while the basic vowel of one word of the riming pair is in the accented syllable, its corresponding syllable is unaccented or half-accented, thus *be-liberty* [1].†
The tendency of this use is to weaken the close of the verse slightly, though when employed in connection

Hunt: The 28 pre-1819 sonnets (exclusive of the *Juvenilia,* since the few youthful attempts at the sonnet included in that volume are stiff, imitative, and non-typical).

Bowles: "At Tynemouth Priory"; "The Bells, Ostend"; "Bereavement"; "Bamborough Castle"; "Hope"; "Influence of Time on Grief"; "Approach of Summer"; "Absence"; "Evening"; "Dover Cliffs."

Wordsworth: "On the Extinction of the Venetian Republic"; "London, 1802"; "I grieved for Buonaparte..."; "Composed Upon Westminster Bridge"; "To the Men of Kent"; "Nuns fret not..."; "Personal Talk, I"; "Methought I saw the footsteps..."; "Now that all hearts are glad..."; "Upon the Sight of a Beautiful Picture"; "Here pause: the poet claims..."; "Ye storms, resound the praises..."; "To B. R. Haydon"; "It is a beauteous evening..."; "The world is too much with us...."

Milton: The 18 English sonnets (exclusive of the caudated example).

Shakespeare: Numbers 1, 10, 18 [20 not typical because every verse has feminine ending], 30, 40, 50, 60, 70, 80, 90, 100, 110, 120, 130, 140.

Spenser: "Amoretti": 1, 10, 15, 18, 20, 30, 40, 50, 60, 70, 75, 80, 88, 89.

*One of Keats's 66 sonnets is unrimed, hence the indication of 65 in this table.

† The theoretical iambic foot tends to pull the emphasis on *ty* into a half-accented position, which still results in the approximate type. Only an overly-mechanical reading would force the syllable into a full-accented position.

with an enjambment line it may form a desirable modulation and enhance the beauty of the rhythm. As with the preceding type, it is in words ending in *y* that we find the most frequent occurrences of this variation, typical examples of which follow: *fragrancy-me* [13]; *tenderly-sea* [32]; *soberly-be* [37]. The following are typical of those not involving the final *y*: *sighs-enterprize* [6]; *pent-firmament* [12]; *things-communings* [27]; *night-Eremite* [59].*

Table VIII, corresponding to that for rimes approximate in sound, indicates the difference in the relative use made of the two types by the writers considered. Comparing the percentage column with that repeated from the preceding table we find that Keats uses a relatively larger percentage of rimes approximate in accent than he does of those approximate in

TABLE VIII

COMPARATIVE TABLE INDICATING USE OF RIMES APPROXIMATE IN ACCENT

Writer	Sonnet Occurrences	Sonnets Considered	Percentage	Percentage Approximate in Sound (Table VII)
Keats	41	65	63	41
Hunt	15	28	53	36
Bowles	2	10	20	30
Wordsworth	9	15	60	60

sound; that Hunt uses slightly more, Wordsworth about the same, but Bowles, less. Keats's higher percentage of approximate accent is probably the result, in part, of his characteristic use of words ending in *y*, eighteen of the forty-one occurrences being of this type. The low percentage for Bowles in each list indicates a strong, well-defined close to his verses.

---

*Justification for assuming that these final, or corresponding medial, syllables were not allowed the theoretical full-accent in the early nineteenth century, is found in Walker's *Dictionary* [*Introduction*, p. 12]: "Verse may sometimes induce a foreigner, as it does sometimes injudicious natives, to lay the accent on a syllable in long words which ought to have none, as in a couplet of Pope's Essay on Criticism:

'False eloquence, like the prismatic glass,
Its gaudy colours spreads on every place.'

Here a foreigner would be apt to place an accent on the last syllable of *eloquence* as well as the first, which would be certainly wrong...."

It is interesting that Milton uses no rimes of this type in the sonnets.

A fourth type of rime found in the works of Keats and others is the *identical*. This term is used to indicate paired words in which not only the emphasized vowel and succeeding elements, but also the preceding consonants, are alike. It includes, but is slightly different from, *rich rime*, in which the two words *(see-sea*[37]) sound exactly alike, but have different meanings. Identical rime applies also to such repetitions as *firmament-languishment* [12], concerning the *ment* of which the question of meaning does not apply. Among additional identical rimes Keats has the following: *veil-prevail* [2]; *light-delight* [7]; *adore-Calidore* [9]; *innocent-sent* [54]. He has also one occurrence of word repetition: *love-love* [66].

A final type of rime correspondence shows an inconsistency between the theory and practice of Leigh Hunt. One of the definitely emphasized points in Hunt's canon regarding the sonnet is that relating to

TABLE IX

COMPARATIVE TABLE INDICATING USE OF VOWEL ECHOES IN NONINTENDED RIME WORDS

Writer	Sonnet Occurrences	Sonnets Considered	Percentage	Percentages for Accent	Percentages for Sound
Keats	29	65	44	63	41
Hunt	12	28	43	53	36
Bowles	7	10	70	20	30
Wordsworth	5	15	33	60	60

the repetition of vowel sounds in nonintended rimes [pl*a*y, g*a*in, refr*a*in, w*a*y].[6] Yet in almost half of the sonnets written by Hunt before 1819 rimes of the type here condemned occur. It is evident that this principle was not made a part of the critic's theory until a time nearer that of writing the "Essay" than that of his contact with Keats. We should not, therefore, expect to find any adherence to this principle in the sonnets written by the younger poet, unless he arrived at and practiced the restraint independently. That he did not will be evident from Table IX and from the following examples: *hail-fail-state-great-fate* [1];

heap-steep-keep-leap-thee-be-flee [5]; *we-week-be-cheek; space-annihilate-haze-dilate* [49]; *placed-taste-haste-waste-away-sway; charm-alarm-heart-part* [54]. One point, however, should be made regarding the evidence for vowel echoes. While occurrences in adjacent quatrains will be evident to most readers, it is questionable if the average reader will retain sounds from, let us say, the first and third verses of the opening quatrain, and be conscious of their echo in the thirteenth and fourteenth verses of the sonnet. Since there are, undoubtedly, readers whose sensitivity enables them to do so, occurrences anywhere within the fourteen verses have been noted.

In the occurrences of vowel echoes it will be noted that Bowles is higher, while Wordsworth is relatively lower, than Keats and Hunt, who agree almost exactly. But of even more interest than the use of single devices is the degree of consistency with which each poet employs his total effects. In a table of this kind, with a relatively small number of items under consideration, a variation of 10 per cent may be discounted. With this allowance, it will be seen that Hunt and Keats, in order, are the most consistent in employing the most frequently occurring rime types with approximately equal emphasis, that Bowles is heavily weighted on the side of vowel echoes in nonintended rimes, and that Wordsworth is consistent in his use of approximate rime, but avoids vowel echoes more successfully than do the others.

From the foregoing we may conclude tentatively (in the absence of exact orthoëpy) that, as compared with writers of his own period, Keats makes use of all types of rime then in vogue, and that, despite a tendency to emphasize rimes approximate in accent, he is reasonably consistent in his employment of the five types. He is seen to be closer to Hunt than to any

other of his contemporaries, in percentage and consistency of use, indicating that not only in general
poetic theory, but also in this aspect of versecraft, the
association was influential. Keats never fully mastered
rime, and the difficulties that caused him to substitute
approximations for exact sounds, or weak for more
exact words, finally led him, late in his poetic life, to
attempt the sonnet experiments. These were designed
to relieve the difficulty, but were at best only moderately successful.

2

What rime is to the vertical pattern of a poem, alliteration and assonance are to its horizontal structure;
and just as unity may be gained by the use of exact
rime, and variety by the introduction of approximate
rime, so alliteration and assonance may contribute to
unity by sound repetitions, and to variety by balance,
or modification, of sound relationships. Frequently
the melodic blend will be so subtle as almost to defy
analysis, but by observing the more objective and well-
defined types of phonetic recurrences, characteristics
of the poet's use may be illustrated. These will suggest
to the reader others of the more subtle elements of
melody which, combined with the rhythmical movement of the poem, account for its oral beauty.

Alliteration is more emphatic than assonance, and
it is, therefore, almost certain to be more obvious.
There is, indeed, some danger that an unskillful use of
the device may cause it to overshadow the thought
development—that the sounds will intrude, and at-
tract more attention than a well-balanced form-content relationship would normally warrant. Many of
the poems of Swinburne are guilty of this. But alliteration is not necessarily an objectionable feature in
poetry. Phrase may be balanced more sharply with

phrase, verse with verse, if the spacing and relative emphasis of the alliterating consonants are carefully controlled. Many times the poet will be scarcely conscious of the use he makes of his sound devices, so long as there is a satisfactory blending when the work is read; but since a subconscious use is as important in its results as is that of a carefully planned technique, and since one of the characteristics of a writer's versecraft is to be found in the skill with which he controls such effects, a study of these devices will be valuable. In order more clearly to illustrate the characteristics of Keats's alliteration, it has seemed desirable to distinguish four types, determined by the positions and number of occurrences of the consonants involved.

First may be considered what we shall call *normal* alliteration, the type in which the nearness of *two* consonants—initial either to the words or syllables, and with at least one in an accented position—causes them to be impressed on the reader's mind as repeated sounds. Obviously, other occurrences of the same sound in noninitial, or in unstressed, positions will add to the melodic value of the verse, but for purposes of distinguishing types it is desirable to limit the sound units to the more emphatic positions. For normal alliteration, as distinguished from the delayed type to be discussed below, the words should be within two or three accents of each other, and the alliterating consonants should register clearly in the mind during a natural reading. A few examples of this most common form will serve to illustrate. First, occurrences within the single verse:

> . . . re*p*entant of the *p*ain [9]

> . . . a victim of your *b*eauty *b*right [37]

> 'Tis not content *s*o *s*oon to be alone [23]

*H*aply a *H*alo round the moon ... [32]

For Jove uncurtain'd Heaven to *l*et thee *l*ive [50]

Another use of normal alliteration results in two verses being bound more closely together, the alliterating sound at the end of one verse being picked up in the opening part of the next, as in the following:

'Tis very sweet to look into the *f*air
And open *f*ace of heaven ... [12]

Round many western islands have I *b*een
Which *b*ards in fealty to Apollo hold [16]

Yet do I often warmly *b*urn to see
*B*eauties of deeper glance ... [26]

We have limited normal alliteration to the occurrence of two similar consonants. A second type, more emphatic than the first, may be called *strong,* in that it is characterized by the presence of three or more like consonants in relatively emphasized positions. Occurrences of the normal type frequently enter the verses in the natural expression of the poet, or because many of our short phrases have become patterned in this way; but if the same sound occurs three or more times it is reasonable to assume that the poet has been conscious of the effect while writing. As with normal alliteration, the strong type may be limited to the single verse, or balanced between two verses. The following will illustrate:

For that to *l*ove, so *l*ong, I've dormant *l*ain [9]

Till the *f*ond, *f*ixed eyes, *f*orget they stare [10]

*F*rom its *f*air *f*ace, shall bid our spirits *f*ly [20]

Made a Nau*m*achia for *m*ice and rats [22]

To question *H*eaven and *H*ell and *H*eart in vain [57]

Its flowery slopes, its river's crystal swell
May seem a span . . . [5]

Or thrice *m*y palate *m*oisten: but when I *m*ark
Such charms with *m*ild intelligences shine [10]

And all his *l*ove for gentle *L*ycid drown'd;
Of *l*ovely *L*aura in her *l*ight green dress [17]

The force of either normal or strong alliteration in unifying and emphasizing phrases or ideas will be evident from the foregoing examples, as will such use in establishing the tone of a given passage. A further use of the device, to which we may give the name *delayed* alliteration, serves a slightly different purpose. In this instance the opening of a verse or phrase may be bound to the end, or the ending of one phrase connected with that of the following phrase, or other situations treated in which it is desirable to retain a given sound at greater distance than with normal or strong alliteration. The distance separating delayed repetition will depend in part upon the effectiveness with which the first consonant is placed, in part upon the skill with which the second is approached, and especially upon the sensitivity of the reader in retaining the first sound. Suggestive examples will illustrate:

O *P*eace! and dost thou with thy *p*resence bless [1]

*F*ull in the smile of the blue *f*irmament [12]

My *s*ense with their deliciousness was *s*pell'd [13]

The *s*tars look very cold about the *s*ky [17]

Why did I *l*augh? I know this Being's *l*ease [57]

How *g*lorious this affection for the cause
Of steadfast genius, toiling *g*allantly [18]

What when a *s*tout unbending champion awes
Envy and Malice to their native *s*ty [18]

Leave *m*elodizing on this wintry day,
Shut up thine olden pages, and be *m*ute [41]

He has his lusty Spring, when fancy clear
Takes in all beauty with an easy *s*pan [48]

In using delayed alliteration involving two verses, Keats frequently falls into a characteristic and interesting balance. He introduces the alliterating consonant with two occurrences in the first verse, thus emphasizing it, and then phrases in such a way that its third occurrence is delayed until approximately the last word of the second verse; or he introduces the consonant with one occurrence in the first verse and emphasizes it with two occurrences in the second. For example:

O Europe! let not *s*ceptered tyrants *s*ee
That thou must shelter in thy former *s*tate [1]

Woman! when I behold thee *f*lippant, vain,
Inconstant, childish, proud, and *f*ull of *f*ancies [9]

For I am brim*f*ul of the *f*riendliness
That in a little cottage I have *f*ound [17]

And their faint *c*racklings o'er our silence *c*reep
Like whispers of the household gods that *k*eep [20]

Forget, in the *m*ist of idle *m*isery,
Life's purposes,—the palate of *m*y *m*ind [66]

Occasionally the delayed alliteration will be involved in three or more verses. Usually a second alliterating consonant will be introduced during this development, but in the following examples only the delayed type has been indicated:

Art thou most lovely?—when gone far a*s*tray
Into the labyrinth of *s*weet utterance,
Or when *s*erenely wandering in a trance
Of *s*ober thought?—or when *s*tarting away [24]*

---

*Note how the *s* sounds in unaccented positions enhance the alliterative effect.

O that a *w*eek could be an age, and *w*e
Felt parting and *w*arm meeting every *w*eek,
Then *o*ne poor year a thousand years *w*ould be,
The flush of *w*elcome ever on the cheek [49]

Standing aloof in giant ignorance,
Of thee I hear and of the *C*yclades,
As one who *s*its ashore and longs perchance
To visit dolphin-coral in deep *s*eas [50]

A fourth type of alliteration employed by Keats may be named *double* from the fact that it balances the recurring sound of one consonant against that of another. This is done in three ways: either by following one set of consonants with a different set, as in the following:

Still *w*arble, dying *s*wan! still *t*ell the *t*ale [2]

*G*ive me a *g*olden pen, and *l*et me *l*ean [23]

O thou whose *f*ace hath *f*elt the *W*inter's *w*ind [47]

or by enclosing one set of consonants with another, as in:

A*tt*uning *s*till the *s*oul *t*o *t*enderness [2]

With careless *r*obe to *m*eet the *m*orning *r*ay [24]

So could we *l*ive *l*ong *l*ife in *l*ittle space [49]

or by alternating the occurrences, as follows:

Hold like *r*ich *g*arners the full-ripen'd *g*rain [42]

From the *n*inth *s*phere to me be*n*ignly *s*ent [54]

*L*et us inspect the *L*yre, and weigh the *s*tress [63]

As with the other types, so double alliteration is used to unify two or more verses, and under these conditions the admission of other sets of consonants frequently results in *multiple* alliteration (three or more consonant sounds). The following will illustrate:

> Or *h*and of *h*ymning angel, when 'tis *s*een
> The *s*ilver *s*trings of *h*eavenly *h*arp atween [23]

> Haply 'tis when thy *r*uby *l*ips part *s*weetly,
> And *s*o *r*emain, because thou *l*istenest [24]

> That is the Grasshopper's—he takes the *l*ead
> In summer *l*uxury,—he is never *d*one
> With his *d*e*l*ights; for when tired out with *f*un [29]

3

Consonants, especially in initial and emphasized positions, have sufficient vocal force to overshadow the vowels which accompany them, with the result that frequently the reader is not aware of the assonating force of the vowel sounds. But assonance, if more subtle, is nevertheless important to the melody of verse, just as the more quiet instrument of an orchestra is important to the tonal effect of a symphony. Poetically, of course, the final effect is a blend of alliteration and assonance, but before considering that aspect of melodic quality, it will be well to characterize types of assonance as we have those of alliteration. The same general patterns of distribution and arrangement may be found in each field (though with relatively fewer occurrences in the case of assonance), and since the foregoing discussion of alliteration will apply—with the substitution of vowel for consonant—to this section, we shall limit ourselves here to examples of each type.

Normal assonance (two occurrences of vowel sound):

> What th*ou*gh, for sh*ow*ing truth to flatter'd state [4]

> Till I heard Chapman speak *ou*t l*ou*d and bold [16]

Let me write down a line of glorious tone [23]

Faded the shape of beauty from my arms [65]

Soft voices had they that with tender plea
Whisper'd of peace ... [13]

O golden tongued Romance, with serene lute!
Fair plumed Syren ... [41]

Strong assonance (more than two occurrences of vowel sound):

May seem a span let me thy vigils keep [5]

The gradual sand that through an hour glass runs [30]

To those who woo her with too slavish knees [61]

       ... I feel a free
A leafy luxury, seeing I could please
With these poor offerings, a man like thee [33]

And yet I never look on midnight sky,
But I behold thine eye's well memory'd light [43]

Delayed assonance (vowel occurrences more widely separated):

A lay that once I saw her hand awake [11]

Life's purposes,—the palate of my mind [66]

       ... and every secret essence there
Reveals the elements of good and fair [27]

Before high-piled books, in charactery,
Hold like rich garners the full ripen'd grain [42]

Double or multiple assonance (two or more sets of vowel sounds in (a) consecutive, (b) enclosing, or (c) alternating order):

(a) Making the triple kingdom brightly smile [1]

   'Tis ignorance that makes a barren waste [44]

   For winds to kiss and grateful bees to feed [62]

(b)   Keep thy chains burst, and boldly say thou art free [1]*

    Let it not be among the jumbled heap [5]

    Still time is fleeting, and no dream arises [31]

    Soft voices had they that with tender plea
    Whisper'd of peace, and truth, and friendliness unquell'd[13]

(c)   He rests at ease beneath some pleasant weed [29]

    The clouds, the trees, the rounded hills all seem [51]

                . . . Great shadow, hide
    Thy face; I sin against thy native skies [51]

4

The reader will have noticed, in the preceding examples, that when only alliterating consonants or assonating vowels were indicated, it was necessary to ignore other sounds in the same verse. This is natural since, except for purposes of study and identification of types, our conception of the melody of a poem is the result not of one or the other, but of a blending of both devices. Before analyzing representative sonnets to determine the total effects of the sound phenomena, however, it may be desirable to indicate certain passages in which the blend of assonance and alliteration is strikingly marked, and to consider other contributing sound phenomena. It will be observed that the alliteration normally dominates the tone value of the passage, but that the assonance offers a nice balance to the emphasized consonants, and accounts in large part for the "fullness" or "richness" that results. The following selections are typical of the balance Keats obtains between these sound devices:

    Let the sweet mountain nymph thy favorite be [1]

    Had I a man's fair form, then might my sighs [6]

---

*Note how the alliterating b tends to overshadow the assonance.

Like a *sick* Eagle *looking* at the *sky* [35]

But, when *I* am consumed *in* the *fire*,
Give m*e* new *Phoe*nix *wi*ngs to *fly* at *my* desire [41]

There *is a* *b*udding *m*orrow *in* *m*idnight,
There *is* a *tri*ple *sight in* *b*lindness keen [50]

5

Occasionally the poet becomes careless in permitting unfortunate sound echoes to appear within the verse in such a way that they intrude upon the reader. Such echoes in the sonnets of Keats are almost uniformly of the type that establish partial or complete rime relationships, either between words within the verse or between a word within the verse and the normal end rime. The effect of this is to anticipate the rime, or make the reader conscious of a riming element in an unexpected position, and so destroy the normal rhythmical balance which is a part of the sonnet pattern. In the following examples only the echoing syllables have been indicated, but the reader will observe that frequently assonance and alliteration increase the effect:

Ah! who can *e'er* forget so *fair* a being [11]

And as it *reach*es *each* delicious ending [23]

Smiling at *eve* upon the quiet *sheaves* [30]

Haply a Halo round the Moon—a *glee*
Circling from *three* sweet pair of Lips in Mirth;
And haply *you* will say the *dewy* birth [32]

Fame, like a wayward Girl, *will still* be coy
To those *who woo* her with *too* slavish knees [61]

6

Refrain and parallelism, while not entirely within the scope of sound devices, have certain of the characteristics of rime, alliteration, and assonance, and show sufficient relationship to account for their inclusion at this point. For just as the devices already discussed contribute to the variety within uniformity of a poem, so unity is gained when an already stated word pattern is repeated in a position where it will be recognized by the reader, and variety is gained by having the repeated elements lead into concepts different from the original, but related in mood or idea.

Normal refrain, in which the entire verse is repeated without change, is used only once in the sonnets of Keats, verses nine and eleven of the unrimed sonnet, number 47, both being

> O fret not after knowledge—I have none;

but refrain of the *incremental* type, wherein something is added—or a different resolution made—in the second occurrence of the verse, is found three times:

> *Happy is England!* I could be content . . .
> *Happy is England!* sweet her artless daughters [26, 1-9]
>
> *The poetry of earth* is never dead . . .
> *The poetry of earth* is ceasing never [29, 1-9]
>
> *Blue! 'Tis the life* of heaven,—the domain . . .
> *Blue! 'Tis the life* of waters:—Ocean [46, 1-5]

It will be observed that incremental refrain as used in the first two instances (both Petrarchan) introduces the octave and the sestet; and that the changed portion of the ninth verse permits the bipartite structure to be maintained nicely. In the third example (Shakespearean), the first two quatrains are opened with incremental refrain, while the opening of the third quatrain is related to the others by parallelism:

> *Blue!* Gentle cousin of the forest-green [46, 9]

The importance of such devices for the maintenance of unity and variety—especially when they are supplemented by rime, alliteration, and assonance—will be evident at once.

Parallelism, closely related to incremental refrain, is one of the most frequently occurring rhetorical devices in the sonnets of Keats. It differs from refrain in that less independent meaning is contained in the repeated words or phrases, these being, in parallelism, introductory to the ideas which follow. For example:

> *Still* warble, dying swan! *still* tell *the tale,*
> *The* enchanting *tale, the tale* of pleasing woe [2, 13-14]

> Minion of grandeur! *think you he* did wait?
> *Think you he* naught but prison walls did see [4, 5-6]

> Haydon! *forgive me that I* cannot speak . . .
> *Forgive me that I* have not Eagle's wings [36, 1-3]

> *Faded the* flower and all its budded charms,
> *Faded the* sight *of beauty from my* eyes,
> *Faded the* shape *of beauty from my* arms,
> *Faded the* voice, warmth, whiteness, paradise [65, 5-6-7-8]

7

While the examples given in the above sections of our study have served to define typical aspects of melody as employed by Keats, they fail to give the larger view which can be obtained only from consideration of the sonnet as a whole. It is, after all, the blending of the previously discussed characteristics that makes the final impression on the reader, and it will assist in bringing the separately treated melodic elements into a more proper relationship if representative sonnets or passages are discussed as units. No attempt will be made to indicate every device used, since such an effort is almost certain to lead to over-emphasis; rather, the aim will be to suggest the key positions of consonants and vowels, and the more striking of the other features.

In the following sonnet, number 24, there is a relatively simple use of sound devices, and it may be well to approach the more complicated through it:

> Nymph of the *downward smile* and *sidelong glance*,   *a*
> In what *diviner moments* of the *day*   *b*
> Art thou *most* lovely?—*when* gone far astray   *b*
> Into the *labyrinth* of *sweet* utterance,   *a*
> Or *when* serenely wandering in a trance   *a*
> Of sober thought?—*or when* starting away   *b*
> With *careless robe* to *meet* the *morning ray*   *b*
> Thou *spar'st* the flowers in thy *mazy* dance?   *a*
> *Haply 'tis when* thy ruby *lips* part sweetly,   *c*
> And *so remain*, because thou *listenest*:   *d*
> But thou to *please wert nurt*ured so com*pletely*   *c*
> That I *can never* tell what mood is best.   *d*
> I shall as soon *pronounce* which Grace more *neatly*   *c*
> *Trips it* before A*pollo* than the rest.   *d*

Several interesting characteristics may be noted in this sonnet. All rimes are exact in sound and without vowel echoes, but *glance-utterance* and *listenest-best* are approximate in accent, and *sweetly-completely-neatly* are of the double or feminine type. In the octave, the verse ends are well defined and emphasized, but in the sestet there is an element of weakness in that four of the six verses end on unaccented syllables. This weakness is modified, however, by the fact that in two cases, *completely* and *neatly*, the verse is of the enjambment type, and the half-accented final syllables lead with rhythmical nicety into the respective succeeding verses. The impression on the reader's ear is satisfactory throughout, since each of the approximate accent rimes *(utterance, listenest)* is followed by a pause, resulting in a natural tendency to emphasize the final syllable slightly. The rime scheme is the one most frequently used by Keats, *abbaabba cdcdcd*, and the balance between form and content is well handled.

Within the verses the sound devices are interestingly

varied and balanced. The *s* sound carries through the first nine verses, but the emphasized *d* and *i* of verse one gradually give way to less emphasized consonants, *l* and *m*, which then come into importance, and so on through the sonnet, one sound giving way to another, frequently to be picked up at a later point, as are both *m* and *l*, where they are placed in relationship with other sounds. There are also echoes within the verses, such as *mo*ments-*mo*st [verses 2-3], *or-mor*ning [5-6-7], *care*less-*spar'*st, *ray-mazy* [7-8], *lips-listenest* [9-10], which do not intrude badly; and *please-wert-nurt*ured-com*ple*tely [11], which do.

Parallelism is also present to such an extent that the entire structure of the sonnet is dependent on it. The series of parallel rhetorical questions all but fill the octave, while the same structure in the form of a statement introduces the sestet, and an approximate parallelism between verses twelve and thirteen brings the sestet to its close.

If the blending of sound in the foregoing example is relatively simple, it is not so in all sonnets, and in the following quatrain (typical of the entire sonnet, number 30) alliteration, assonance, and rime present an extremely complicated blending of effects:

> After *d*ark *v*apors have o*pp*ress'd our *pl*ai*n*s
> *For* a long *dreary* se*a*son, *c*omes a *day*
> *Born* of the *g*entle South, and *c*lears aw*ay*
> From the *s*ick h*ea*vens all uns*eemly* st*ai*ns . . .

An analysis of these verses shows that whereas in sonnet number 24, just discussed, each consonant and vowel was fairly sharply defined as it was introduced, in the present example the sounds are more or less buried in their surrounding consonants and vowels, and emerge gradually, frequently in company with two or three others which must be carried along at the same time. Add to this the fact that all rimes of the octave have the same vowel sound, and a maximum of complication results. The verses will be taken in order:

After *d*ark *v*apors have *opp*ress'd our *pl*ains

The initial *d* of *dark* is to be picked up in verse two, but the *a* and *p* of *vapors* are echoed within the verse, the latter by the double *p* of *oppress'd*, and then both, but in reverse order, in *plains*. At this point of echo, however, another sound is introduced, the *l* of *plains*, to be emphasized in verse two. More than this, the word *oppress'd* introduces a blend of *pr*, the *r* of which, with the preceding *d* of *dark*, enters into *dreary* in the next verse. There are, then, two sounds, *a* and *p*, at least partially satisfied in verse one, and three, *d*, *r*, and *l*, introduced but retained for balance until the following line. Verse two then gives us:

For a *l*ong *dreary* se*a*son, *c*omes a *d*ay

Here, as the three consonants, *d*, *r*, and *l*, are satisfied, others closely associated with them are introduced. The *d* of verse one is given strong support by its double occurrence in verse two, but as it is read in *dreary* it blends into what is almost a rime with *clear* in verse three. Indeed, the *ear* of *dreary*, the *l* of *long*, and the *c* of *comes* all (if we may anticipate) enter into the formation of the sound of *clear* in the following verse. More than this, the initial position of *For* in verse two and *Born* in the following verse creates a definite echo, and the *sea* of *seasons* is to be strongly supported in the succeeding verses. Verse three then follows:

Born of the gentle South, and *clears* aw*ay*

The opening word gives us the echo of *For* in the preceding verse. Then a less obvious short *e* in *gentle* may be retained by the reader (if he does not become lost in the maze of other effects) until the similar position of *heaven* in verse four satisfies it. The *s* of *South* picks up the sound from the preceding verse and anticipates its further extension in that which follows; *clears* fulfills the anticipation already discussed, and the long *a* of *away* continues the vowel echo in non-intended rimes of the octave. The quatrain then closes:

> From the sick heavens all unseemly stains

after which the strengthened *s* is permitted to rest temporarily (until verse ten) ; the short *e* of *gentle* in verse three is satisfied in *heaven;* the repeating rime echo of long *a* finds its fourth rime occurrence in *stains;* and the long *e* of *unseemly* picks up *seasons of* line two and anticipates *relieved* in verse five.

An analysis of the remaining verses of the sonnet would reveal a continued blend of alliteration and assonance, the main features of which have been indicated. There is, of course, no reason to believe that Keats, as he wrote, was conscious of the intricacy with which these sounds intertwine; but he was undoubtedly conscious of the alliteration and assonance in the key positions, as his use in other sonnets attests; and the presence of such a large amount of repetition as we have here, while exceptional, is at the same time illustrative both of the possibilities and dangers present in using such devices.

The two sonnets quoted have illustrated, respectively, a simple and an extreme use of melodic devices. A third type, dependent rather on quality than quantity, in which certain sounds give a unified tone value to the entire sonnet, should also be noted. The harshness of the *s* sound, which occurs so frequently in English, is liable to dominate any poem unless carefully controlled. Keats was reasonably successful in this regard, and in the following sonnet, number 17, there is only one alliterating occurrence of *s* (verse three), and the much softer *l*, supported by a nicely balancing *f*, gives the tone to the sonnet as a whole. These sounds are well suited to the mood of the poem, and are most pleasing when the sonnet is read aloud. Parallelism will be observed as an integral part of the structure, beginning with verse five:

> Keen, fitful gusts are whisp'ring here and there
> Among the bushes half leafless, and dry;
> The stars look very cold about the sky,
> And I have many miles on foot to fare.
> Yet feel I little of the cool bleak air,
> Or of the dead leaves rustling drearily,
> Or of those silver lamps that burn on high,
> Or of the distance from home's pleasant lair:
> For I am brimful of the friendliness
> That in a little cottage I have found;
> Of fair-hair'd Milton's eloquent distress,
> And all his love for gentle Lycid drown'd;
> Of lovely Laura in her light green dress,
> And faithful Petrarch gloriously crown'd.

In comparing the melody of Keats's sonnets in any general way with that of the other sonnets considered, one is liable to step outside the bounds of objectivity; for much depends on whether one happens to enjoy an abundance or a minimum of sound emphasis, and whether his ear is sensitively attuned to the finer shadings. Our limitation of illustrative examples to Keats's poems should not be permitted to overstress his characteristics; if a similarly complete treatment were feasible for all of the poets with whom his work has been compared, it would undoubtedly lead to the conclusion that these devices are among the writer's finest tools.

As with all fine tools, however, care must be exercised in their use, and in this it is questionable whether

Keats was as successful as the others. The beauty of
certain passages is too frequently countered by a harshness that—in the light of the perfection found in the
odes—can only be ascribed to inexperience or carelessness. And since intrusive echoes are found in the
late as well as in the early sonnets, it would seem that
the poet's most serious melodic fault was the latter.

III. Metrical Variations

The one condition for writing a sonnet about which
there has been almost no disagreement since the form
was introduced, is that it shall have as its framework
fourteen basically iambic pentameter verses. Through
these the idea is developed, and into their structure
the devices for sound are woven. But the term "basically iambic" suggests once more our frequently emphasized principle of variety within uniformity, carried now, however, into the very movement of the
verses, and made an inherent part of them; for if all
verses were invariably iambic pentameter the result
could be only a singsong monotony. Using the iambic
as the basic foot, therefore, variants, in the form of
modified or substituted feet, will be permitted to relieve the theoretical monotony of the pattern. Similarly, using the pentameter as the basic verse, either
longer or shorter verses will, rarely, be admitted, or
variety will be given by using enjambment verses,
pauses within the line, feminine endings, or similiar
effects, as modifications of the exactly measured five-
foot verse.

The present division of our study will deal with the
variations employed by Keats (and those with whom
he is compared) in heroic meter as adapted to the
sonnet. Determination of the most satisfactory reading of a verse is, of course, difficult, because of the

individuality of expression that will accompany interpretation. For purposes of analysis in this section an effort has been made to give the sonnets a natural reading that suggests the meaning as the present writer interprets it; to permit normal accentuation balanced by the theoretical pattern to determine the relative emphasis of syllables in a polysyllabic word; and to emphasize the words that carry the idea forward where a grouping of monosyllabic words makes such distinction necessary. Half accents, which indicate shadings of emphasis, have, for sharper definition of effects, been converted in this section into the unaccented or accented markings to which they most nearly approximate; and in general an attempt has been made (for comparative purposes) to bring the readings into conformity with those applied by Lucien Wolff to the blank verse and heroic couplets of Keats.[7]

1

Since the normal iambic pentameter is the theoretical basis of the sonnet, it will be well to establish first the degree in which it is made a part of the poems under consideration. There is, of course, no reason why the poet should attempt to maintain the theoretical heroic meter, since variety is desirable; but it is possible to suggest a limit of variation beyond which the integrity of such a verse is jeopardized. If the establishment of such a point is not taken too literally (since many considerations must enter into a reading) we may assume that, since the pentameter is made up of five feet, at least three of these should be iambics if the normal movement is to be maintained, and that two variant feet, therefore, will not destroy the integrity of the verse. It is the problem of the poet to balance lines that might be mechanical, if given in too large numbers, with those more freely varied, and to maintain a relationship between them that will be pleasing to the reader.

By a normal verse is meant one in which the natural reading (but ignoring half accents) results in the accented and unaccented syllables falling into the theoretical iambic pentameter pattern, as in the following:

> When thou art dead, and all thy wretched crew [4]

Verses in which certain of the feet are varied may be typified by the following:

> God! she is like a milk white lamb that bleats [11]

in which foot one is a trochee (or inverted iamb) and foot four a spondee; or

> The ocean with its vastness, its blue green [15]

in which the present reading finds pyrrhics in the second and fourth feet, and a spondee in foot five. The relationship between Keats and the other writers considered, with regard to numbers of feet varied in sonnet verses, will be indicated by Table X.* Since the number of poems considered is not the same for each writer, greater clarity has been sought by converting the actual numbers of verses into percentages of the total lines considered. The nonsonnet percentages for Keats have been computed from Wolff's figures.

The table presents some interesting suggestions. Dealing first with the normal verses, we note that the evidence points to a gradual increase, historically, of freedom in the use of heroic verse in the sonnet. Whereas Spenser and Shakespeare follow the iambic pentameter most closely, and Milton in only slightly less degree, the nineteenth-century poets show a definitely greater freedom. Of the latter group, the negligible difference between the percentages of Keats and

Hunt is consistent with their relationship in the non-sonnet poetry, where Wolff finds that "regular lines occur ... seldom in both poets."[8] In Keats's general poetry, however, there are only about 10 per cent normal verses, indicating that in the quatorzains, where the percentage is 14, a greater restraint results from use of the sonnet form.

TABLE X

COMPARATIVE TABLE INDICATING VERSES IN WHICH DIFFERENT NUMBERS OF FEET ARE VARIED

[by percentages of total verses]

Type	Keats nonsonnet	Keats sonnet	Hunt	Bowles	Words-worth	Milton	Shake-speare	Spenser
Normal	10	14	12	16	11	22	24	24
One foot varied	not given	34	35	41	39	39	34	49
Two feet varied	32	36	36	34	37	28	30	22
Three feet varied	17	14	14	6	11	9	8	5
Four feet varied	3	2	2	1	2	2	3	0
Normal plus one foot varied	....	48	47	57	50	61	58	73
Normal plus one plus two feet varied	....	84	83	91	87	89	88	95

*Verses altered in all five feet are, of course, rare. In the sonnets Keats has only one; Hunt, two; Milton, one; and, in those analyzed, Shakespeare, one. In the nonsonnet poems of Keats, studied by Wolff, that writer finds nine occurrences in fourteen hundred and two verses, or less than 1 per cent.

The figures for lines varied in only one foot present a slightly altered relationship between the writers, however, there being less discrepancy among the group. This is to be expected, inasmuch as most writers are not concerned particularly with keeping their verses mechanically normal—indeed, are rather more concerned with preventing that condition—and the moderately varied line will be the more frequently used. Spenser, it will be observed, has a much larger percentage of verses of this type than has Shakespeare, while, in turn, Shakespeare uses a greater number of lines with two feet varied. In the percentages for verses altered in two and three feet, we note again the growing flexibility of the heroic verse, for Shakespeare, Spenser, and Milton all employ considerably smaller percentages of verses that contain the larger numbers of variants, than do the nineteenth-century writers. A striking exception to this, however, is Bowles, whose average of verses varied in three feet is close to that of the Elizabethans.

As to the relationship between Keats and Hunt, it will be evident at once that the association of the two writers resulted in allied habits of verse structure. They are consistently in agreement in every phase of the table (the differences of 1 or 2 per cent being negligible), and with no other poets of the group is there any approximation to the same consistency. Both Keats and Hunt show more restraint in their use of the sonnet form than they do in their general poetry, the figures from Wolff for Keats's blank verse and couplet poems being typical. It will be noted that the percentages of verses in which the integrity is maintained (two feet varied) is higher in the sonnets, while in those with the greater variations (three or more feet varied) the sonnet percentages are lower, than in the blank verse and couplet poems.

A word should be added concerning the totaled figures, indicating comparisons for verses in which normal plus one variant, and normal plus one plus two variants, are shown. Once more Bowles is seen to be close to the Elizabethans in the regularity of his structure—almost equal to Spenser, in 95 per cent of whose verses (of those analyzed) the integrity is maintained. The other writers range between 83 and 89 per cent, figures that lead to the conclusion that, if the poets are representative sonneteers, the use of the restricted form will lead the average writer to employ a fairly high percentage of regular or only slightly modified verses in his sonnets.

A more specific indication of the use of relatively normal verses is possible by determination of the particular verses in which the type occurs. Is there, for example, a tendency to regularize the verses as the division points of the sonnet are approached, or do the regular verses occur at haphazard? Table XI, in which the normal verses plus those varied in one foot have been used as the basis, will show this distribution for what may be considered as a typical (or com-

TABLE XI

COMPARATIVE TABLE INDICATING RELATIVELY NORMAL VERSE DISTRIBUTION
[by percentages of total verses]

	Verse													
	1	2	3	4	5	6	7	8	9	10	11	12	13	14
Keats	35	41	48	49	49	43	65	58	48	49	45	51	34	57
Hunt	46	39	50	75	36	43	54	57	43	46	57	57	50	43
Bowles	70	80	60	50	50	30	70	70	80	50	30	60	40	70
Wordsworth	47	33	47	47	73	33	40	60	67	47	53	27	53	67
Milton	39	39	61	61	56	56	67	61	78	72	72	67	56	67
Shakespeare	60	47	53	53	40	67	60	73	60	73	40	33	87	67
Spenser	60	67	80	80	80	53	87	87	60	93	67	67	60	73

posite) sonnet for each writer. As Keats is quite consistent in this distribution in both the Italian and Shakespearean sonnets, they have been grouped together.

In the table the higher percentages have been italicized for each writer, and it will be observed that there is a marked individuality in the employment of regular and irregular verses. Keats, for instance, permits his typical sonnet to open with a line that is comparatively free in relationship to the other verses; he then increases the rigidity of the verse at the closing of the first and opening of the second quatrain, and employs his greatest regularity as the octave (or second quatrain in the Shakespearean examples) close is approached in verse seven and reached in verse eight; he then falls back into his general use until verse thirteen, where the greatest amount of freedom is permitted, after which he closes the sonnet with a fairly regular verse. Hunt, on the other hand, opens with more regularity than does Keats, and, unlike Keats, shows his greatest rigidity of line at the close of the first quatrain, a very high percentage of regular lines occurring at that point. He then re-establishes the integrity of the verse as he approaches the octave close. In the sestet he has a peculiar characteristic: verses eleven and twelve are written with regularity comparable to that of the octave close, but the sonnet is permitted to end on a relatively irregular verse, in which only 43 per cent of the cases have as few as one foot varied. Characteristics for the other poets will be clear if reference is made to the table.

The point of closest agreement among the writers is found in the tendency to steady the sonnet movement in verses seven and eight, regardless of the pattern used—thus strengthening the structure, or emphasizing its bipartite nature—and to close the sonnet with a fairly regular movement. One would expect a higher percentage of regular opening verses, since the reader orients himself to the pattern of the poem at this point; but, with the exception of Bowles, Shakespeare, and Spenser, approximately regular initial verses occur in less than 50 per cent of the examples studied. This may be accounted for by reference once more to the growing freedom in use of the heroic verse, the exception in the case of Bowles being consistent with his general closeness to the technique of the Elizabethans.

Spenser is by far the most regular in his employment of the approximately normal verse in all positions; Milton, Shakespeare, and Bowles (in that order) are next; and Hunt, Wordsworth, and Keats permit the largest numbers of irregular verses.

We may consider the sonnets written before March, 1817 (at the beginning of which month the 1817 volume was published), as composed while Keats was an apprentice to his art; and those of March, 1817, and after as the more mature evidence of his expression. By this date the influence of Hunt was waning, and Keats was writing with greater integrity to his own style. Coincidentally, the sonnets divide numerically (in Finney's chronology) almost exactly at March, 1817—the first thirty-four are dated between 1814 and February, 1817, while the last thirty-two begin with March, 1817—and Table XII presents a comparison of Keats's use of normal and varied lines in the two periods (but with a division of thirty-three against thirty-three for comparative purposes).

TABLE XII
TABLE INDICATING KEATS'S USE OF VARIANTS BEFORE AND AFTER
MARCH, 1817

Type Verse	Occurrences early period	Occurrences late period	Percentage increase or decrease
Normal	64	69	Increase 8
One foot varied	172	139	Decrease 20
Two feet varied	160	175	Increase 12
Three feet varied	57	64	Increase 8
Four feet varied	9	12	Negligible
Five feet varied	1	0	Negligible

This table shows that, while Keats increased slightly the number of regular verses in the later period, he employed, at the same time, a larger percentage of those verses which are varied in more than one foot, and a smaller percentage of those varied in only one foot. This, we may assume, is consistent with the increasing maturity of the poet—as he masters his technique he is free to admit, and more skillful in admitting, verses of greater variety, while he is likewise better able to control the normal verses when they are essential to the movement of the sonnet, and more exact in holding them to the theoretical pattern.

2

In addition to knowing the degree of variation that is to be found in the verses, it is desirable to determine also the position in which the variant is used. In theory at least, it would seem better, except for special emphasis, to modify the opening rather than the closing feet of the verse, since the unevenness that might result from the variation in theoretical pattern would then have time to modulate into the more regularly moving passage. Table XIII illustrates what has actually been done in the sonnets examined. The nonsonnet percentages for Keats have again been compiled from Wolff's figures.

TABLE XIII

COMPARATIVE TABLE INDICATING OCCURRENCES OF VARIANTS BY FEET

[by percentages of total verses]

	Keats nonsonnet	Keats sonnet	Hunt	Bowles	Words-worth	Milton	Shake-speare	Spenser
Variations in foot one....	54	49	45	41	50	40	38	31
Variations in foot two....	31	25	26	23	27	20	19	18
Variations in foot three..	37	30	37	28	31	28	29	33
Variations in foot four....	31	30	26	26	25	27	27	16
Variations in foot five....	18	20	22	10	17	15	19	10

Examination of this table bears out the theoretical assumption made in the preceding paragraph: with the exception of Spenser (whose sonnets present a negligible discrepancy), all of the writers have used a significantly larger percentage of variant occurrences in foot one. An apparent contradiction of the principle involved is presented by the fact that foot three rather than foot two is second in frequency of variations, and that in the case of Keats, Bowles, Milton, and Shakespeare, foot four is approximately equal to foot three in such frequency. This can be explained by the equally important theoretical assumption that the poet will not normally invite roughness by immediately following one variation with another; he will rather vary, let us say, the first foot, return to the normal iambic for the second and possibly the third foot, and then permit a second variation to occur, returning finally to the normal iambic in foot five or in feet four and five. This procedure would maintain the smoothness of the verse and at the same time space the variations in such a manner that variety within uniformity would result.

The relatively small percentage of variation in foot five, in the case of Bowles and Spenser, can be accounted for by the absence or scarcity, respectively, of feminine endings in the sonnets examined. The discrepancy between the nonsonnet poems and the sonnets of Keats is in agreement with our earlier findings, and may be ascribed to the more rigid demands of the sonnet form. Again it will be observed that the relationship between Keats and Hunt is very close, though in this instance Keats and Wordsworth are more nearly parallel in their percentages.

3

Possibly more important than either the number or position of variants in each verse is the question of the kind of variant used by the poet. On this depends the degree of strength or weakness, of smoothness or roughness, which characterizes the poem as a whole when it is read. It is important also to know in which foot or feet each type variant occurs, since, as we have seen, the effect of variants on the reader is, in part at least, dependent on position.

In an iambic verse the principal types of variation will be those resulting from what is, in effect, the substitution of other feet for the normal iambic, or from an added unaccented syllable to form feminine ending. Table XIV is designed to indicate both the type of variant used, and its frequency of occurrences in the different feet. The totals will suggest the comparative cumulative use of the given type by each poet.

The table shows that in general the writers are rela-

tively equal in their use of the more important variants. Exceptions in the sonnets examined, however, are
found in Wordsworth's high percentage of pyrrhics,
in Spenser's low percentage of spondees and trochees,

TABLE XIV*

TABLE INDICATING TYPE VARIANTS AND OCCURRENCES IN DIFFERENT FEET
[by percentages of total verses]

Foot	Keats nonsonnet	Keats sonnet	Hunt	Bowles	Words-worth	Milton	Shake-speare	Spenser
				Pyrrhic				
1	11	8	10	6	10	7	10	9
2	11	9	10	10	12	7	8	6
3	21	19	22	18	23	19	17	25
4	16	18	18	15	17	12	12	8
5	6	7	5	2	8	5	6	6
Total	65	61	65	51	70	50	53	54
				Spondee				
1	16	14	12	14	17	11	9	9
2	17	14	16	11	13	12	11	10
3	10	7	9	6	5	7	6	4
4	10	9	4	10	4	11	11	7
5	10	7	9	8	7	6	7	3
Total	63	51	50	49	46	47	44	33
				Trochee				
1	25	22	22	21	23	22	18	13
2	2	1	0	1	1	0	0	1
3	4	3	5	4	2	2	5	4
4	4	2	4	0	1	2	4	2
Total	35	28	31	26	27	26	27	20
			Feminine Ending					
5	see note	5	7	0	2	4	6	1

in Bowles's failure to use feminine endings, and in
Wordsworth's and Spenser's scarcity of such endings.
   One important bit of evidence concerning the
Keats-Hunt relationship is contained in the table.
Wolff draws the following conclusion from his study
of the 1817 volume:

*Wolff finds 20 per cent feminine ending in the 1817 volume, 4 per cent in
"Endymion," 0 per cent in the "Epistle to John Hamilton Reynolds," and
"Lamia," and 2 per cent in "Hyperion." In the sonnets Keat shows a definite
decrease in the second period, with only twelve feminine ending occurrences,
against thirty-six before 1817. The pyrrhic endings in the sonnets are more
evenly distributed, twenty-seven occurrences before 1817, and thirty-four after.
   In addition to the variants represented in this table, syllabization results frequently in anapests, in numbers (irrespective of feet) as follows: Keats, 35;
Wordsworth, 9; Milton, 4; Shakespeare, 1; Spenser, 2. The dactyl is used only
once by Keats (and only once in the nonsonnet poetry) and not at all by the
others. Keats uses the amphibrach six times in the early sonnets (before number 30), as compared with one occurrence each for Milton and Hunt.
   Two words, "heaven" and "flower," have been considered monosyllabic in
the following (brackets enclosing line numbers): 10[5]; 11[13]; 12[3]; 13[5];
23[2]. Keats's use justifies this, but since with one exception the words occur
before pauses, they should be noted as possible amphibrachs.

Keats exaggerates Hunt's frequent habit of introducing a trochee at the first foot, and a pyrrhic at the 3rd and 4th, and thereby gives his verse a limping gait.[9]

If these variants and their positions will be observed in respect to the sonnets, it will be seen that Hunt is exactly even with Keats in trochees used in foot one, exactly even in pyrrhics in foot four, and that he uses 3 per cent *more* pyrrhics than Keats in foot three. Keats is thus more regular in this aspect of his sonnet structure than is Hunt, but so closely allied in all the figures that the relationship between the two is again emphasized.

From the table it is evident also that the normal position for the most frequent use of the pyrrhic foot as variant is in foot three (balancing the verse nicely), and in each instance the highest percentage is found at that point; that the spondee falls most naturally into either the first or second foot (opening the verse with strength, or phrasing to an emphasized second foot); and that the trochee is one of the most frequently used of all variants, and consistently so in foot one. It will be seen later that this use of the trochee (or inverted iambic) in foot one permits one of the most desirable phrasing patterns in the heroic meter, since the verse opens with strength and returns usually to the normal iambic movement with the second foot, thus permitting the verse to smooth out easily and with rhythmical nicety after a strong opening.

Keats's response to the more rigid structure of the sonnet is again evident from the comparative figures, and there is in almost every instance a more frequent use of variants in the general poems written in heroic verse.

4

A conclusion reached through the preceding table is that, with such consistency as was shown in num-

bers, types, and positions of variants, certain typical
verse patterns should result. An analysis of the total
verses considered bears out this implication and shows
that seven patterns clearly leading all others in frequency of occurrence may be considered basic to the
sonnets as a whole. In Table XV the verse type is
indicated by allowing its initial letter to represent the
variant foot, and the number which follows it to represent the position in the verse. Thus, *p3* means that a

TABLE XV

TABLE INDICATING MOST FREQUENTLY OCCURRING VERSE PATTERNS

[by percentages of total verses]

Type	Keats	Hunt	Bowles	Words-worth	Milton	Shake-speare	Spenser
Normal	14	12	16	11	22	24	24
p3	6	6	7	7	5	4	17
t1	5	6	8	6	7	6	6
s1	4	4	8	9	4	3	5
p4	5	6	4	4	5	2	3
p2	3	2	6	3	2	1	3
t1 p3	3	3	1	3	2	2	3

pyrrhic foot is substituted for the iambic in foot three,
the other feet being normal iambics; and *t1 p3* indicates that a trochee has replaced the iambic in foot one,
while a pyrrhic occupies foot three of the same verse,
the other feet being normal iambics. Representative
verses showing the nature of these variations as they
actually occur in the sonnets, may be helpful. The
following illustrate, in order of importance for the
group of writers, the seven most frequently occurring
verse patterns:

Normal: When thou art dead, and all thy wretched crew [4]

　　p3: And many glor*ies of* immortal stamp [28]

　　t1: *Musing* on Milton's fate—on Sydney's bier [14]

　　s1: *Fair plum*ed Syren, Queen of far-away [41]

　　p4: And each imagin'd pinn*acle* and steep [35]

　　p2: 'Tis ig*norance* that makes a barren waste [44]

　t1 p3: *Happy* and thought*less of* thy day of doom [53]

The table will indicate the percentage of frequency for these verse patterns.*

As in the earlier tables, so here the normal verse is seen to be the one most frequently used. Steadiness of the movement demands this, and the same principle accounts for the fact that five of the six remaining typical patterns involve only one variant each. Although the general closeness in percentages suggests that these seven patterns are the most generally employed in heroic verse (as used in the sonnet), there are certain individual characteristics that may be noted.

It will be observed that once more the figures for Keats are throughout closer to those of Hunt than to any other of the group—that, therefore, even in the matter of verse phrasing, the influence is clear. Of the others, Spenser is abnormally high in his percentages of pyrrhics substituted for the third foot, almost to a degree (subject to analysis of all his sonnets) that a phrasing habit is suggested. Bowles and Wordsworth are relatively high in their percentage of spondees in the opening foot; and Bowles makes a more frequent use of the pyrrhic in foot two than do the others.

5

A final type of variation, different in principle from the foregoing, is that in which the verse is either shortened or lengthened. There are three general ways in which this violation of the sonnet norm may occur: the poet may consciously employ an unbalanced line; he may, through failure to revise carefully, unconsciously permit such a verse to remain in an otherwise balanced sonnet; or, as most frequently happens, he

---

*Next in frequency are the following, not distributed among the writers with sufficient evenness, nor high enough percentages, to warrant conclusions: *s2*; *p1 s2*; *s5*; *t1 p4*; *s4*; *p1*; *s1 p3*; *p3 s4*; *t1 s2*.

may phrase the ten syllables of his verse in such a manner that they combine to form not five, but four feet — decasyllabic tetrameter or heroic tetrameter. It is sometimes possible to read the heroic tetrameter in such a way that the shortened verse is not noticeable or intrusive; usually, however, the syllabic rearrangement forms two anapests, and results in a lightness of movement out of keeping with the normal iambic. The following will illustrate the type:

Of sober thought?—or when starting away [24]

In the sonnets examined, only Shakespeare and Milton invariably use the true pentameter. Hunt and Bowles have two hexameters each; Wordsworth has two heroic tetrameters; and Spenser, two hexameters and one heroic tetrameter. With the larger number of sonnets analyzed for Keats, there will naturally be more frequent occurrences, but the following list will indicate that in a relative consideration also, he is much freer in the use of nonpentameter verses than are the others. The sonnets of the first period account for eleven (60 per cent) of the nineteen occurrences. The verse number is enclosed in square brackets, and line numbers questioned are debatable or susceptible of two readings:

Dimeter: 21[3].

Tetrameter (normal): 2[7].

Tetrameter (heroic): 8[1]; 10[4?]; 12[4]; 17[2?]; 24[6]; 31[5?, 8]; 35[13]; 36[13]; 45[4]; 50[13?]; 58[1].

Hexameter: 1[14]; 13[14]; 41[14]; 54[7?]; 58[14].*

Heptameter: 1[9].

---

*Hexameters predominate in closing verses, possibly the result of a Spenserian stanza influence.

IV. Phrasing

Variety within uniformity is furthered not only by the devices considered in the earlier sections of our study, but also by the manner in which the poet phrases his ideas within the fourteen-verse iambic pentameter structure. If units of thought, measured to the five-foot line, occur in large numbers, stiffness or monotony will result; if too great freedom is permitted, the movement will be characterized by looseness or jerkiness. The problem of the poet in controlling these conditions is to employ his phrasing devices in such a way that, like Milton, he finds "the sense variously drawn out from one verse into another," thus giving "true musical delight."[10]

1

Our principal concern in dealing with the phrasing characteristics of a poet is to know how he might have read his lines aloud—where, and with what degree of definiteness, the pauses would have occurred. But we are immediately faced with a handicap equal to that encountered in dealing with approximate rimes; for it was, in many instances (and particularly so before the nineteenth century), the compositor and not the writer who determined the punctuation to which we must go for evidence—and we can be no more certain of how, for example, Spenser or Shakespeare might have punctuated their sonnets, than we can of how they might have pronounced many of their rime words. Three courses are open to us. We may repunctuate all of the sonnets in conformity with modern principles; we may take one poet (Keats) as a standard, and bring the others into agreement with him; or we may eliminate from any but incidental consideration those who seem to have had little part in the final punctuation of their works. The first two of these methods obviously fail to give the evidence predicated by the aim of this section. But we are reasonably secure in proceeding with the third line of attack.

We know, for instance, that Hunt, as a publisher, would be acceptably dependable in the matter of punctuation, and that Keats, in associating with him, might reasonably assimilate certain of the other writer's habits—especially so since the mutual reading of poems, and the criticisms by Hunt, noted earlier, would offer opportunity for such influence. That Keats himself, while careless in the unpublished sonnets, was concerned about the correctness of his published work, is evident from his statement regarding a review published in *The Champion*. He writes:

> ... the one they have put in is so badly punctuated that you perceive I am determined never to write more, without some care in the particular.[11]

Again, he makes a detailed set of corrections, with suggestions on the relationship between punctuation and meaning, in discussing the printing of "Endymion" with Taylor.[12]

Hunt and Keats, then, should be (and a comparison of their sonnets shows them to be) reasonably in agreement. Wordsworth, too, in the sonnets examined, punctuates in such a way that there is acceptable consistency with that for Keats and Hunt. We may, then, determine comparisons for these three writers, but should remember that, despite every care to arrive at an objective standard of judgment, all comparative figures must remain suggestive rather than final, and tentative conclusions, given in the notes, are all that can be reached for the others. For Keats, however, it is not difficult, despite his erratic methods, to determine intent, and the definite pauses are, in most instances, easily distinguished from those less emphasized.

In the following tables two degrees of pause have been considered—those relatively weak (comma pauses), and those comparatively strong. For the latter, Keats uses several indications—exclamation points, semicolons, colons, long and short dashes, or combinations of these.

We may note first the degree to which the poets allow the ends of verses to coincide with phrase or sentence conclusions, *i. e.* to result in conventional end-stopped lines. If the number of such verses is considered in relation to the total lines, the following comparative percentages result: Keats, 36; Hunt, 30; and Wordsworth, 43. Wordsworth, that is to say, exhibits a tendency to close the phrase at the verse end more frequently than do the others. Hunt and Keats differ more widely in this than in other characteristics, but in an interesting manner; for Keats, who is generally supposed to have emulated, and even exaggerated, the laxness of Hunt, is more regular in the matter of closing the verse conventionally. Indeed, he shows a nice balance in his use of end-stopped and enjambment verses, with avoidance both of stiffness and looseness. It is interesting to note also that in every instance more than 50 per cent of the verses are of the run-on, or slight comma pause, type.*

A further aspect of end-stopping may be indicated by determining the relative distribution of such pauses. This is shown in Table XVI, which reveals certain individual characteristics. Keats pauses most frequently (disregarding the necessary final pause) at the end of verse eight, with 91 per cent in this position.

---

*Corresponding percentages for the other poets may be suggested tentatively as follows: Bowles, 32; Milton, 29; Shakespeare, 46; and Spenser, 44.

One might have expected the poet to be influenced to some degree by the comparative freedom with which Milton manages the octave close, but the fact that Hunt has an eighth-verse pause in 100 per cent of the sonnets known to Keats explains the latter's regularity. Hunt's influence is therefore re-emphasized, but here only to the extent of determining a generally bipartite structure; for in other positions, and especially at the end of verse four, the two poets differ

TABLE XVI
COMPARATIVE TABLE INDICATING DISTRIBUTION OF END-STOPPED VERSES
[by percentages of total verse occurrences]

					Verse									
	1	2	3	4	5	6	7	8	9	10	11	12	13	14
Keats	28	28	6	74	15	22	6	91	23	35	20	42	17	100
Hunt	7	14	14	36	29	4	7	100	36	18	18	25	11	100
Wordsworth	33	33	27	60	27	20	40	80	27	53	33	40	33	100

widely in practice. Independent habits are thus quite naturally exhibited by Keats in the less general aspects of phrasing.

Keats's next most frequent pauses occur at the ends of verses four and twelve (though only one third of the occurrences in verse twelve are in Shakespearean sonnets); Wordsworth emphasizes the pause at the ends of verses four, eight, and ten; while Hunt is high (40 per cent or more) only at the octave close, where the invariable pause occurs.*

In general (though comma pauses tend to invalidate the conclusion) enjambment verses will occur in lines other than those dominated by end-stopping. The following percentages of such verses in all lines considered will, therefore, apply more particularly to the lines with the lower percentages in Table XVI: Keats, 32; Hunt, 26; and Wordsworth, 24. Keats thus uses

---

*For the others, as determined by thought development, the following characteristics are suggested: Bowles, 50 per cent or more at the ends of verses 4, 5, 9, and 12; Shakespeare, invariable pauses at the ends of verses 4, 8, and 12, and 50 per cent or more at verses 2, 6, and 10 [indicating thought development in two-verse units]; Spenser, comparable with Shakespeare. Milton is so varied in use of end pause that in only one instance, verse 8 (owing to some consistency in the early sonnets), does the percentage rise as high as 40.

more enjambment verses (his general average is from four to six per sonnet) than do the others. In his nonsonnet poems, however, Keats's percentage is 43, indicating greater restraint in the sonnet.*

A final consideration relating to the verse close has to do with the syllabic pattern of the final foot. Substitution of an anapest for the iamb does not alter the movement materially, since the rising meter is maintained. Similarly, a spondee in the final position merely emphasizes the strength of the verse end. Substitution of a trochee wrenches the meter so sharply that it is, as we have seen, usually avoided in foot five. But by using the feminine ending, or by substitution of a pyrrhic (the last syllable of which will normally be

TABLE XVII

COMPARATIVE TABLE INDICATING USE OF FEMININE AND PYRRHIC ENDING

[by percentages of total verses]

Keats nonsonnet sonnet		Hunt	Bowles	Words-worth	Milton	Shake-speare	Spenser
Feminine Ending							
See note to Table XIV	5	7	0	2	4	6	1
Pyrrhic Ending							
6	7	5	2	8	5	6	6

given a half accent) for the iambic, modification in the verse close can be obtained. In each instance, however, the line is completed on an unaccented syllable and, unless care is exercised to lead the phrasing through this pattern and into the next verse, desirable emphasis may be lost.

Table XVII shows the relationship between the writers† in the use of these variants, with the nonsonnet figures again based on Wolff. The low percentages throughout the table indicate that these devices are more sparingly used than are some of those

---

*Of the others, Spenser and Shakespeare have very few enjambment verses, 11 and 12 per cent (though comma intrusions undoubtedly prejudice the figures) ; Milton, as might be expected, is highest, with 39 per cent ; and Bowles is moderate, with 29 per cent.

† Including Spenser, Shakespeare, Milton, and Bowles, since the problem is one of scansion rather than punctuation.

already studied, or that they occur as admitted exceptions to the normal technique. As to individual use, the pyrrhic is the most consistently employed by the writers as a group, while the feminine ending involves considerable discrepancy. Keats holds almost a norm position in relationship to the others, and is approximately even with Hunt, Milton, and Shakespeare. Bowles, Wordsworth, and Spenser are surprisingly low, although a wider examination of Spenser's sonnets suggests a figure nearer 4 per cent as being applicable to the "Amoretti" as a whole.

2

The importance of the verse close for phrasing has been shown in the analysis just completed. Both writer and reader are constantly progressing towards this position, and its emphasis is increased by the slight pause resulting from the necessity of returning the eyes to the beginning of the following verse. Of slightly less importance, therefore, but at the same time susceptible of varied placement denied to the end pause, is the medial pause. The point at which it occurs is less important than that variety be maintained; normally, however, a definite caesura after an initial syllable or foot which has been approached through an enjambment verse, will be avoided, since it comes too abruptly for smoothness, as in the following:

> How many mice and rats hast in thy days
> Destroy'd? [40]

The question of whether the pause follows an accented or an unaccented syllable, thus forming, respectively, a masculine or feminine caesura, will clearly be as important as that relating to masculine and feminine ending, and in Table XVIII comparisons for these and other types of medial pause are listed. Since there is a natural tendency to hesitate slightly at the end of each verse, regardless of punctuation, the comma pause is less important at that point than it is within the line, where a marked emphasis is contributed to the phrasing. Characteristic lines will indicate the types of medial pause with which we are concerned:

Masculine caesura: Complete my joy—let not my first wish fail [1]

Feminine caesura: Thou sweetly singest; naught thy hymning mars [3]

Masculine comma pause: And while, for rhymes, I search around the poles [20]

Feminine comma pause: In noisome alley, and in pathless wood [18]

Keats averages eight medial pauses for each sonnet; Hunt, eleven; and Wordsworth, ten.* Since the figures for Keats include both periods, it should be stated that after 1817 he shows a slight tendency to decrease the number of feminine caesurae, and to increase all other types of medial pause. Greater emphasis is placed

TABLE XVIII
COMPARATIVE TABLE INDICATING USE OF MEDIAL PAUSES
[by percentages of total internal pauses]

Type	Keats	Hunt	Wordsworth
Feminine caesurae	16	6	12
Masculine caesurae	17	10	18
Feminine comma pauses	22	30	31
Masculine comma pauses	43	53	40

on the masculine pause, both in caesura and comma positions, throughout the later period. This illustrates the natural tendency to strengthen poetic structure as the writer masters his craft. As between the sonnets and nonsonnet poems, the average of eight pauses for each sonnet is overbalanced by twelve for each four-

*For the other poets, Spenser averages only three; Shakespeare, seven; Milton, eight; and Bowles, ten.

teen lines of the general poetry, suggesting that longer phrases are used in the quatorzains.

Conclusions suggested by the table may be drawn briefly. For medial pauses of all types the three writers are approximately equal. The use of feminine caesurae, however, is seen to be largely an individual matter, with Keats nearer to Wordsworth than to Hunt in this regard. Wolff finds the device used "seldom" in the general poetry,* but in the sonnets the feminine caesura is a definite characteristic of Keats's verse, and gives an easily recognized close to many of his phrases.

The figures for masculine caesurae again show Keats more in agreement with Wordsworth—indeed, with the exception of the feminine comma pause, Keats is, throughout this table, closer to Wordsworth than to Hunt.

A sonnet, number 46, illustrating the foregoing types of verse close and medial pause, will show the manner in which the devices become a part of general sonnet structure:

Blue! 'Tis the life of heaven,—the domain	1
Of Cynthia,—the wide palace of the sun,—	2
The tent of Hesperus, and all his train,—	3
The bosomer of clouds, gold, grey and dun.	4
Blue! 'Tis the life of waters:—Ocean	5
And all its vassal streams, pools numberless,	6
May rage, and foam, and fret, but never can	7
Subside, if not to dark blue nativeness.	8
Blue! Gentle cousin of the forest-green,	9
Married to green in all the sweetest flowers,—	10
Forget-me-not,—the Blue bell,—and, that Queen	11
Of secrecy, the Violet: what strange powers	12
Hast thou, as a mere shadow! but how great,	13
When in an Eye thou art, alive with fate!	14

*It is difficult to interpret Wolff's figures for caesurae since his readings do not indicate the pauses. If my interpretation of his material is correct, the following relationship is established: caesurae of both types are involved in 20 per cent of sonnet verses, and in 11 per cent of nonsonnet verses. Keats thus phrases to the medial pauses more frequently in the sonnets than in the general poetry.

The problem of phrase length will be discussed in the next section, but we may follow through the movement of the poem here, giving principal attention to the medial and end pauses. The one-syllable exclamation, "Blue!" opens the verse with strength and splits the inverted foot, the masculine caesura being compensated for in the next phrase by the lightness of what is, in effect, an anapest (*'Tis the life*). The phrase then closes with a feminine caesura (*heaven*), balancing the earlier occurrence of the masculine type. Picking up with a lightness of touch that emphasizes the earlier anapestic pattern, there follows the enjambment phrasing that leads into what is, through elision, a feminine caesura (*Cynthia*), and the second verse then closes with a masculine end-stop (*sun*). Thus the strength of the masculine pause is balanced by the relative weakness inherent in the feminine pauses. The first three phrases are approximately equal (three and four feet) in length, but the fourth phrase (*The tent . . . train*), with a slight feminine comma pause to break its movement, coincides exactly with verse three. The fourth verse balances the third except that it has two comma pauses, both masculine, and a slightly modified metrical pattern (a pyrrhic and a spondee). Verse five, involving incremental refrain, parallels the opening line, in that only a part is occupied by the phrase (*Blue! . . . waters*), the second caesura (*waters*) being feminine as in verse one. And again a run-on verse (including a forced pronunciation of *ocean* to avoid a tetrameter) carries into the following line—now, however, with a long, sweeping phrase that is not concluded definitely until the pyrrhic ending (*nativeness*) of verse eight. This sixteen-foot phrase is broken up by slight comma pauses which give variety, and prevent an uncomfortably long and "breathless" effect in reading. Parallelism with the first and fifth verses then splits the initial foot of line nine, a masculine caesura *(Blue!)* resulting, but this time the following phrase picks up on an accented syllable and carries through an end-of-verse comma pause to a feminine ending *(flowers)* at the close of the following line. Then two short phrases, with masculine *(not)* and feminine *(Blue bell*)* caesurae alternating, are followed by a run-on line that carries through another comma pause to the feminine caesura *(Violet)* in verse twelve; and this in turn is followed by an enjambment verse with feminine ending *(powers)*, which leads to a feminine caesura *(shadow)* in verse thirteen. Finally, with comma pauses intervening, the sonnet closes with a masculine ending *(fate)*, giving excellent strength after the large number of feminine devices with which the verses are supplied.

This sonnet is a good illustration of the manner in which it is possible to play off one effect against another: longer phrases against shorter, end-stopped lines against enjambment, comma pauses against caesurae—so blending that a pleasing variety within uniformity results. Such effects are only slightly less subtle than those for melody; and the interactions of sound, metrical variations, and phrasing, actually *are* the sonnet to the extent that a poem is dependent on versecraft.

3

The sonnet just considered has illustrated the variety of phrase lengths the poet must employ in order to prevent monotony. It has shown also that the length of a sentence or phrase which offers a complete section of thought *(i. e.* a caesura- or end-stopped phrase), will usually be modified by comma pauses, metrical

---

*Bell may, of course, be given a half or even a full accent.

variations, or different types of verse close. With the last two we have already dealt in detail, and we may note here the comparative use made by the poets of phrases of all types—from comma to comma, from comma to caesura, from caesura to end-stop, etc.

In Table XIX the seven most widely used phrase lengths (by feet) are given in their order of frequency for the three writers whose punctuation can be compared.* Of these phrase lengths it is natural

TABLE XIX

COMPARATIVE TABLE INDICATING MOST FREQUENTLY-OCCURRING PHRASE LENGTHS
[by percentages of total phrases]

	Phrase Length in Feet						
	5	*2*	*3*	*1*	*2½*	*1½*	*½*
Keats	24	10	10	9	8	5	6
Hunt	16	13	14	12	8	8	4
Wordsworth	20	13	10	11	8	5	9

that the most frequently occurring should be determined by the verse pattern, since the poet will normally tend to think in approximate conformity to the basic pentameter.† One might reasonably expect, however, that the five-foot length would be broken, more frequently than the figures indicate, by comma pauses, leading to a predominance of shorter phrases. Since this is obviously not the case, it may be suggested that the verse (in this case pentameter) chosen by the writer will determine the length of from 20 to 25 per cent of his phrases.

Next in importance (but on an average with less than half as many occurrences) are the phrases of two and three feet length, followed by extremely short two-syllable phrases that vary the movement of longer units. Then occur the phrases which divide one

*The Elizabethans, as might be expected, seem more strict in holding to the five-foot phrase, with Milton and Bowles more nearly equal to Keats, Hunt, and Wordsworth. Spenser is unusually high in phrases of ten feet, and low in those of one, and one and a half, feet. Otherwise, discrepancies are negligible.

† Not that the phrase coincides with the heroic verse in every instance. The phrasing habit becomes established so that in many instances the five-foot phrase divides, without pause, between two verses.

or more of the feet involved, either by beginning after a pause has split the preceding foot, or by closing with a feminine pause.

Of the individual characteristics, it may be noted that Keats and Wordsworth are more regular than Hunt in conforming to the pentameter norm, the latter showing a slight preference for the shorter phrases. In the later period Keats exhibits a tendency to shorten the phrases, as is consistent with increasing maturity and mastery of the medium.

Of the larger units of phrasing—end-stopped phrases or sentences, without regard to intervening comma pauses—there are three types: those (by far the larger number) which open at the beginning of the verse, and close either medially or at a verse end;

TABLE XX

CAESURA- OR END-STOPPED PHRASES OR SENTENCES OPENING WITH
BEGINNING OF VERSE

[by percentages of total phrases of this type]

	Verses							
	½	1	1½	2	2½	3	3½	4
Keats	14	21	9	25	5	6	2	13
Hunt	14	19	8	9	6	9	1	19
Wordsworth	13	39	5	24	8	5	1	5

those which open within the verse, and close at the *end* of the same or a following verse; and those which open within the verse, and close in a *medial* position within one of the following verses.

Table XX offers comparative figures for the predominant lengths in the first type. For convenience in listing the types, and since figures for general rather than exact phrase lengths are desired in this instance, any segment of a verse—whether one foot or four—has been called one-half. It will be noted that there is extreme individuality in the use of these type phrases.* Keats prefers, in order, phrases that fill the equivalent of two, one (with an increase in its use in

---

*The Elizabethans are especially high in two-verse phrases. Milton and Bowles are in agreement with Keats and Wordsworth for such phrases. Wide discrepancies are found throughout the other lengths, however.

the second period), one-half, and four verses; Hunt those occupying one, four, and one-half verses; and Wordsworth, one, two, and one-half.*

For the second and third types (phrases opening medially), occurrences are so few as to make percentage figures misleading. In general, it may be stated that when the phrase opens within the verse, it will be carried most frequently through to the end of the next verse (a phrase of one and one-half verses). If this is not done, the tendency is to shorten the phrase and end it at the close of the verse in which it begins. The third choice is to carry it through the next *two* complete verses,† or, occasionally, through the next three. When the phrase is started within the verse and ends within the next verse, it is almost uniformly carried only through five feet. Keats is in complete agreement with all of these tendencies.‡

4

We have considered metrical variants in an earlier discussion, but only as to types and positions in the verse. Now, with the backgrounds of general phras-

*Bowles prefers, in order, phrases that fill two, four, one, and three verses; Milton, two, four, and three; Shakespeare, two, one, and four; and Spenser, two and four.

† This type, illustrated by the lines
                    . . . Pale were the sweet lips I saw,
            Pale were the lips I kiss'd, and fair the form
            I floated with, about that melancholy storm [58]
is a favorite with Keats for closing the Shakespearean form. See numbers 42, 43, 46, 47 [unrimed], 55, and 58.

‡ The first ten lines of the "Chapman's Homer" sonnet are made up entirely of two-verse phrases, with only one (the first) varied by a comma pause. I would suggest that this resulted from composition in Keats's mind while walking home from Clarke's rooms. The poet might naturally "block out" material in these larger sections (compare number 17, written under similar conditions). The last four verses are nicely varied—an enjambment line which pauses at a medial caesura, a balancing phrase which then opens medially and closes at the end-stopped thirteenth verse, and finally, a one-verse phrase which closes the sonnet. It is natural that most of the commentary on this sonnet relates to the magnificent close, for Keats has not entirely escaped the danger inherent in five consecutive two-verse phrases. That the average reader is not conscious of monotony may be ascribed in part to the interest created in the ideas, and accompanying strength of imagery; but in part also to the fact that, while the larger phrase divisions are unfortunately parallel, the monotony is relieved by the inclusion of many variants that alter the iambic movement of the verse and contribute variety to the extreme uniformity.

ing developed, it is possible to indicate how certain phrase patterns are established through their use. An element of strength, for example, will be given the phrase if its opening is marked by an accented syllable, as in the following:

> Surely the mind of man is closely bound [28].

This may be accomplished by inverting the opening iambic (as here), by substituting a spondee, or—since the phrase may begin within the line—by having it follow a phrase that has just closed on a feminine caesura, as in

> Thou sweetly singest: naught thy hymning mars [3].

Normally, of course, the initial syllable of the phrase will be unaccented, since the meter is iambic, but the extent to which the stronger opening has been used by the writers considered may be observed in Table XXI. It will be noted that Keats and Wordsworth are about equal in a relatively high percentage of the accented type, while, except for Spenser, the others are quite consistent. The figures for Keats's two periods indicate a slight tendency to increase the strong opening in his later period.

TABLE XXI

COMPARATIVE TABLE INDICATING RELATIVE STRENGTH OF PHRASE OPENING
[by percentages of total phrases]

	Keats	Hunt	Bowles	Words-worth	Milton	Shake-speare	Spenser
Unaccented	61	68	70	59	70	69	79
Accented	39	32	30	41	30	31	21

By limiting ourselves to the brief phrase, or phrase segment, that includes the metrical variant and thus gives variety to the movement of the line, it is possible to indicate the patterns most consistently used by the writers as a group. This method has a further advantage since it will suggest the variants best suited to the iambic pentameter verse in whatever stanza form it may be used, for these phrasing techniques are the normal means of avoiding monotony in the heroic meter.

The most frequently used patterns are four in number, and the relationship between them and the metrical variants discussed earlier will be evident. First in importance is the phrase type / x x /, illustrated by the phrase "Who can forget" [11], and characterized by a strong opening which returns to the normal iambic immediately.* It should be noted that a slight change in the length of a phrase, while it will not destroy the effect of the basic pattern, may modify it to a point where a related (rather than a basic) pattern will result. For example, "This is your birthday" [20] is the foregoing basic pattern with an unaccented syllable added—giving, in effect, a feminine close— and is therefore a related pattern. Of this first type Keats uses the basic arrangement 140 times in the sonnets, with 100 additional uses in closely allied formations.

Next in importance is the pattern x / x x x /, illustrated by the phrase "To regions of his own" [4], in which the pyrrhic modulates the movement. This pattern is used 108 times by Keats, with 124 additional related uses. The third most frequently employed phrase pattern is / / x /, illustrated by "Small, busy flames" [20], with the spondee giving the variety, and used by Keats 103 times basically, with 87 related uses. Type four reverses this pattern, giving x / / /, as in "the great man's fame" [18], and is used 60 times by Keats, with 34 occurrences of related patterns.

*The words of the phrase will not necessarily coincide with metrical variations in the feet, since the phrase may open on the second syllable of a foot that has been divided by a caesura. In effect, of course, a phrase opening after a fairly strong pause becomes, in reading, closely related to one coinciding with the verse opening. There are, naturally, many phrase patterns besides those given here, but they do not occur with sufficient frequency to represent general tendencies.

Of these and other less significant variant patterns the following averages per sonnet prevail: Spenser, 12; Shakespeare, 13; Milton, 13; Wordsworth, 16; Bowles, 15; Hunt, 16; and Keats, 16. The larger numbers for the later writers again confirm the gradual change evident in the handling of heroic verse. With the smaller number of variants, the sonnets of Shakespeare, Spenser, and Milton naturally have a steadier, more regular movement.

The greatest consistency of use by the group as a whole is to be found in the distribution of these four types, indicating that they are the variants most natural to heroic verse. In certain other, less frequently used, patterns there is considerable discrepancy, the result of individual habits of phrasing, and these are in each instance consistent with the differences in the use of metrical variants discussed earlier. Thus, Wordsworth's frequent use of the anapest results in phrase patterns that are frequently dominated by this metrical variant, while Keats's use of the pyrrhic ending makes an iambic followed by a pyrrhic one of his favorite subtypes.

Conclusion

Praise or blame has but a momentary effect
on the man whose love of beauty in the ab-
stract makes him a severe critic of his own
works.

[Letter to James Hessey,
October 9, 1818]

I refused to visit Shelley that I might have
my own unfettered scope;—and after all, I
shall have the reputation of Hunt's élève.
His corrections and amputations will by the
knowing ones be traced in the poem.

[Letter to Benjamin Bailey,
October 8, 1817]

CONCLUSION

The analyses and discussion of the foregoing study have established the principal characteristics of sonnet versecraft as employed by Keats. We may now, in the light of the evidence adduced, formulate a more general estimate of the poet as one in the group of writers considered.

In general, Keats followed sonnet custom as he knew it. The early nineteenth century had as its most popular and best established quatorzain the Italian form. The Spenserian had almost disappeared from use, and the Shakespearean, after a rapid development in popularity among the lesser writers of the closing eighteenth century, had yet to find its first significant champion—after Shakespeare—in Keats himself. But the Shakespearean pattern was adopted by Keats only after approximately forty of the sixty-five sonnets had been written with conservative adherence to the Petrarchan form. Invariably, in the latter pattern, the poet used the rigid *abbaabba* octave, and his favorite sestet schemes were the universally acceptable *cdcdcd* and *cdecde*. Even when he turned to the English form, the technique developed in his use of the Italian pattern was transferred with little change except conformity to the different rime scheme.

If, however, Keats was conservative in his use of the forms he employed, he was not slavish. In adapting content to structure, he did not force his ideas into the pattern, but achieved a nice balance between the two elements; and as early as the second extant sonnet, there is evidence of a desire to alter the rigid structure, which he felt to be uncongenial to the English language. After this early attempt, however, he returned to the conventional Italian pattern until,

with growing confidence and independence, he felt
ready to make use of the Shakespearean. Once the
transition was made, he tried, on five different occasions, to alter the accepted forms by changes in rime
scheme. Three of these were, in effect, a blend of two
Shakespearean type quatrains with an Italian type
sestet. But, owing to unfortunate rime correspond-
ences, the experimental sonnets were only moderately
successful.

Keats's knowledge and theory of the sonnet are
not difficult to trace. There was little in the contemporary or eighteenth-century opinion regarding
the quatorzain that would guide the young writer in
mastering its structure, but the poet could, and apparently did, go, if not to the Italians, to the models
of such writers as Shakespeare, Milton, Wordsworth,
and, especially, Leigh Hunt. The influence of the
latter has been shown clearly to be dominant in
Keats's versecraft; for, granting the possibility of
mutual influence, we have seen that not only were the
general poetic theories of the two parallel, but even
in matters of rhythmical variants, pattern choice, and
similar characteristics of technique, Keats was much
closer to Hunt than to any other of the writers considered. Indeed, the percentages are at times so
markedly parallel as to be unequivocally convincing.
When Hunt was not followed, there was a minor influence from Wordsworth, in certain of the more
obvious devices—such as rime types and strong phrase
openings—that would naturally be carried over from
the enthusiastic reading we know Keats to have given
the older poet's work.

In following these writers, the poet exhibits characteristics of versecraft that indicate their influence,
and, at the same time, shows individual qualities that
distinguish his work from that of the sonneteers with

whom he has been compared. If he is judged by the larger aspects of sonnet knowledge possessed by nineteenth-century poets—rather than by that of twentieth-century purists—he is seen to be thoroughly in agreement with the backgrounds of sonnet writing known to him. He used, it is true, devices that are frequently criticised today—identical rimes, rimes with vowel echoes in unrelated positions, rimes approximate in sound and (most frequently) in accent—but there was ample precedent for such use, and the poet should not be condemned for techniques that were an established part of sonnet tradition in his age.

Characteristic elements of the poet's versecraft may be summarized briefly. In his use of normal or approximately normal verses, he is consistent with the frequency of such lines in early nineteenth-century sonnets—relatively fewer than in the Elizabethan examples—and his tendency is to close quatrains, octaves, and sestets with these regular verses. This use emphasizes the divisional structure of the poem, and, combined with a relatively large percentage of phrases opening with accented syllables, gives general strength to his work. In position of variants in his lines, also, Keats is highly consistent, and follows the representative use of such devices, with occurrences most frequent in foot one, three, or four. In this use he agrees more closely with Wordsworth than with Hunt, as is shown by the detailed figures. For types of variants, as well as for the verse patterns resulting from their use, Keats, again in remarkable agreement with Hunt, conforms to tradition. But in verses with larger numbers of variants, and in lines longer or shorter than the pentameter, he is relatively high.

In regard to the verse close, end-stopping is used conservatively by the poet, his percentage being practically the norm figure for the group as a whole. The full pause is found almost invariably (91 per cent) at the close of verse eight; and relatively high numbers of such pauses at the ends of verses four and twelve suggest a tendency to organize the thought in quatrain units. Enjambment, while used by Keats with greater frequency than by any other of the writers except Milton, is, nevertheless, employed with greater restraint than in his nonsonnet poetry. This fact suggests that the discipline demanded by the form caused the poet, in some degree, to overcome the license so often exhibited in his heroic couplets. The other devices—feminine and pyrrhic endings—relating to the verse close, are used by Keats with a generally acceptable and unintrusive distribution.

In the use of medial pauses, and in phrase lengths resulting from them, the poet conforms, with one exception, to a normal distribution for the group. The exception is his characteristic employment of the feminine caesura, which will be observed by the reader as a definite influence on the verse phrasing, particularly if the sonnets are read aloud. Of the larger phrase lengths (ignoring comma pauses), Keats prefers, when the phrase and verse opening coincide, those (in order) of two, one, one-half, and four verses. If the phrase opens medially, he conforms to the general tendency for lengths of one and one-half, one-half, and two and one-half verses—for phrases that carry to ends of lines—and one verse for phrases that both begin and end medially. And as variants to the dominant iambic movement of these phrases, he uses most frequently the patterns / x x /, x / x x x /, and / / x /, in agreement with the use of the writers as a group.

For the most part, alliteration and assonance are well balanced in the sonnets, and increasingly so in the second period, and this balance contributes in many instances to the effectiveness of phrases in which the devices are used. But, probably because he lacked opportunity or care for revision, unfortunate sound echoes frequently intrude. Nor is the fault limited to the early sonnets, for the sensitive ear of the poet— as evidenced by the melodic beauty of the odes—seems not to have been sufficiently attuned to the tonal errors present throughout the range of his sonnet writing. It is, however, incorrect to assume that, because of such difficulties, Keats abandoned the quatorzain. We are justified only in suggesting that the ode structure became the emphasized medium for expressing ideas that might otherwise have been treated in sonnets—not that it replaced the form.

In many ways, however, the quatorzains seem to have been the training ground where Keats prepared himself for the perfection found in the odes, but not, as Professor Garrod has contended, because of the relationship in rime schemes. A far deeper significance attaches to the technical mastery of the poetic tools that has been evidenced—particularly when the sonnets of the early period have been compared with those written after 1817—in the progress of our study. At times, certainly, the poems are metrically rough, but it should not be forgotten that many of them were considered poetic "sins" by Keats himself, and that had care been expended on their revision a different body of material might be present to us. But even with the evidence as it is, we see the craftsman learning his art. At those points where regularity or strength is essential to unity of impression, Keats is usually the equal or superior of his contemporaries; and where variety can be admitted without loss of artistic effect, his sonnets are amply varied.

The sonnet offered a challenge to the poet, a challenge of discipline, restraint, and conformity to the

demands of an artistically perfected medium. It was
a challenge not present in any of the other forms
used by Keats in his early period of writing; for in
the couplets particularly, following Hunt's urge to
escape from the stiffness of the Popean school, the distinction between freedom and license was not always
recognized, and mere looseness—the antithesis of art
—resulted. This was scarcely possible in a form be-
hind which there was the tradition and prestige, among
those whose works Keats knew, of Spenser, Shakespeare, Milton, and Wordsworth; and while the poet
several times gave evidence of being restive with the
rigid demands—and in the experimental sonnets tried
to escape the more irksome—he did, nevertheless, continue to employ the form throughout his poetic life.

As we compare the sonnets of the closing period
with those written before March, 1817, we find a
richer blend of variety within uniformity, and a more
skilful adaptation of content to form—the two goals
towards which all poets strive. And with the confidence thus gained from mastery of this most restricted
of English structural patterns, Keats turned to the
odes, and carried to them a deftness of touch and a
sureness of technique that marked them, in a sense,
the masterpieces which followed the technical apprenticeship of the sonnets.

Appendix I:

The Complete Sonnets of John Keats

Here are the poems. They will explain
themselves, as all poems should do without
comment.

[To George and Georgiana, 1819]

THE TEXT OF THE SONNETS

In the following grouping of the complete sonnets of Keats, the chronology determined by Claude Lee Finney *(The Evolution of Keats's Poetry)* has been followed, as it was in the body of the present study. The text of sonnet number 64, first published in Mr. Finney's work, has been reprinted here by permission of the Pierpont Morgan Library.

Sonnet number 27, first published in Amy Lowell's *John Keats,* follows her printing by permission of Houghton Mifflin Company.

Sonnet number 67, transcribed from shorthand by H. W. Garrod, and included in his *The Poetical Works of John Keats* (Oxford University Press, 1939), was first printed in the *Times Literary Supplement* for November 27, 1937, but appeared too late to be incorporated in the technical phases of the present study. The sonnet is, however, thoroughly consistent with the characteristics of versecraft discussed above, and would in no way alter the conclusions there reached, except to change the number of Shakespearean sonnets to sixteen, and the total number to sixty-seven. This sonnet has been reprinted by permission of Oxford University Press.

The other sonnets follow the text of H. Buxton Forman's *The Poetical Works of John Keats,* and have been reprinted by permission of Oxford University Press.

1. ON PEACE

O Peace! and dost thou with thy presence bless
The dwellings of this war-surrounded Isle;
Soothing with placid brow our late distress,
Making the triple kingdom brightly smile?
Joyful I hail thy presence; and I hail
The sweet companions that await on thee;
Complete my joy—let not my first wish fail,
Let the sweet mountain nymph thy favourite be,
With England's happiness proclaim Europa's Liberty.
O Europe! let not sceptred tyrants see
That thou must shelter in thy former state;
Keep thy chains burst, and boldly say thou art free;
Give thy kings law—leave not uncurbed the great;
So with the horrors past thou'lt win thy happier fate!

April, 1814

2. TO BYRON

Byron! how sweetly sad thy melody!
Attuning still the soul to tenderness,
As if soft Pity, with unusual stress,
Had touch'd her plaintive lute, and thou, being by,
Hadst caught the tones, nor suffer'd them to die.
O'ershadowing sorrow doth not make thee less
Delightful: thou thy griefs dost dress
With a bright halo, shining beamily,
As when a cloud the golden moon doth veil,
Its sides are ting'd with a resplendent glow,
Through the dark robe oft amber rays prevail,
And like fair veins in sable marble flow;
Still warble, dying swan! still tell the tale,
The enchanting tale, the tale of pleasing woe.

December, 1814

3.   TO CHATTERTON

O Chatterton! how very sad thy fate!
Dear child of sorrow—son of misery!
How soon the film of death obscur'd that eye,
Whence Genius mildly flash'd, and high debate.
How soon that voice, majestic and elate,
Melted in dying numbers! Oh! how nigh
Was night to thy fair morning. Thou didst die
A half-blown flow'ret which cold blasts amate.
But this is past: thou art among the stars
Of highest Heaven: to the rolling spheres
Thou sweetly singest: naught thy hymning mars,
Above the ingrate world and human fears.
On earth the good man base detraction bars
From thy fair name, and waters it with tears.

January, 1815

4.   WRITTEN ON THE DAY THAT MR. LEIGH HUNT LEFT PRISON

What though, for showing truth to flatter'd state,
Kind Hunt was shut in prison, yet has he,
In his immortal spirit, been as free
As the sky-searching lark, and as elate.
Minion of grandeur! think you he did wait?
Think you he naught but prison walls did see,
Till, so unwilling, thou unturn'dst the key?
Ah, no! far happier, nobler was his fate!
In Spenser's halls he stray'd, and bowers fair,
Culling enchanted flowers; and he flew
With daring Milton through the fields of air:
To regions of his own his genius true
Took happy flights. Who shall his fame impair
When thou art dead, and all thy wretched crew?

February 3, 1815

5.

O Solitude! if I must with thee dwell,
Let it not be among the jumbled heap
Of murky buildings; climb with me the steep,—
Nature's observatory—whence the dell,
Its flowery slopes, its river's crystal swell,
May seem a span; let me thy vigils keep
'Mongst boughs pavillion'd, where the deer's swift leap
Startles the wild bee from the fox-glove bell.
But though I'll gladly trace these scenes with thee,
Yet the sweet converse of an innocent mind,
Whose words are images of thoughts refin'd,
Is my soul's pleasure; and it sure must be
Almost the highest bliss of human-kind,
When to thy haunts two kindred spirits flee.

November, 1815

6. TO ————

Had I a man's fair form, then might my sighs
Be echoed swiftly through that ivory shell
Thine ear, and find thy gentle heart; so well
Would passion arm me for the enterprize:
But ah! I am no knight whose foeman dies;
No cuirass glistens on my bosom's swell;
I am no happy shepherd of the dell
Whose lips have trembled with a maiden's eyes.
Yet must I dote on thee,—call thee sweet,
Sweeter by far than Hybla's honied roses
When steep'd in dew rich to intoxication.
Ah! I will taste that dew, for me 'tis meet,
And when the moon her pallid face discloses,
I'll gather some by spells, and incantation.

February or March, 1816

7.

As from the darkening gloom a silver dove
Upsoars, and darts into the Eastern light,
On pinions that naught moves but pure delight,
So fled thy soul into the realms above,
Regions of peace and everlasting love;
Where happy spirits, crown'd with circlets bright
Of starry beam, and gloriously bedight,
Taste the high joy none but the blest can prove.
There thou or joinest the immortal quire
In melodies that even Heaven fair
Fill with superior bliss, or, at desire
Of the omnipotent Father, cleavest the air
On holy message sent—What pleasures higher?
Wherefore does any grief our joy impair?

February, 1816

8.

How many bards gild the lapses of time!
A few of them have ever been the food
Of my delighted fancy,—I could brood
Over their beauties, earthly, or sublime:
And often, when I sit me down to rhyme,
These will in throngs before my mind intrude:
But no confusion, no disturbance rude
Do they occasion; 'tis a pleasing chime.
So the unnumber'd sounds that evening store;
The songs of birds—the whisp'ring of the leaves—
The voice of waters—the great bell that heaves
With solemn sound,—and thousand others more,
That distance of recognizance bereaves,
Make pleasing music, and not wild uproar.

March, 1816

9.

Woman! when I behold thee flippant, vain,
Inconstant, childish, proud, and full of fancies;
Without that modest softening that enhances
The downcast eye, repentant of the pain
That its mild light creates to heal again:
E'en then, elate, my spirit leaps, and prances,
E'en then my soul with exultation dances
For that to love, so long, I've dormant lain:
But when I see thee meek, and kind, and tender,
Heavens! how desperately do I adore
Thy winning graces;—to be thy defender
I hotly burn—to be a Calidore—
A very Red Cross Knight—a stout Leander—
Might I be loved by thee like these of yore.

April or May, 1816

10.

Light feet, dark violet eyes, and parted hair;
Soft dimpled hands, white neck, and creamy breast,
Are things on which the dazzled senses rest
Till the fond, fixed eyes, forget they stare.
From such fine pictures, heavens! I cannot dare
To turn my admiration, though unpossess'd
They be of what is worthy,—though not drest
In lovely modesty, and virtues rare.
Yet these I leave as thoughtless as a lark;
These lures I straight forget,—e'en ere I dine,
Or thrice my palate moisten: but when I mark
Such charms with mild intelligences shine,
My ear is open like a greedy shark,
To catch the tunings of a voice divine.

April or May, 1816

11.

Ah! who can e'er forget so fair a being?
Who can forget her half retiring sweets?
God! she is like a milk-white lamb that bleats
For man's protection. Surely the All-seeing,
Who joys to see us with his gifts agreeing,
Will never give him pinions, who intreats
Such innocence to ruin,—who vilely cheats
A dove-like bosom. In truth there is no freeing
One's thoughts from such a beauty; when I hear
A lay that once I saw her hand awake,
Her form seems floating palpable, and near;
Had I e'er seen her from an arbour take
A dewy flower, oft would that hand appear,
And o'er my eyes the trembling moisture shake.

April or May, 1816

12.

To one who has been long in city pent,
'Tis very sweet to look into the fair
And open face of heaven,—to breathe a prayer
Full in the smile of the blue firmament.
Who is more happy, when, with heart's content,
Fatigued he sinks into some pleasant lair
Of wavy grass, and reads a debonair
And gentle tale of love and languishment?
Returning home at evening, with an ear
Catching the notes of Philomel,—an eye
Watching the sailing cloudlet's bright career,
He mourns that day so soon has glided by:
E'en like the passage of an angel's tear
That falls through the clear ether silently.

June, 1816

13. TO A FRIEND WHO SENT ME SOME ROSES

As late I rambled in the happy fields,
What time the sky-lark shakes the tremulous dew
From his lush clover covert;—when anew
Adventurous knights take up their dinted shields:
I saw the sweetest flower wild nature yields,
A fresh-blown musk-rose; 'twas the first that threw
Its sweets upon the summer: graceful it grew
As is the wand that queen Titania wields.
And, as I feasted on its fragrancy,
I thought the garden-rose it far excell'd:
But when, O Wells! thy roses came to me
My sense with their deliciousness was spell'd:
Soft voices had they, that with tender plea
Whisper'd of peace, and truth, and friendliness unquell'd.

June 29, 1816

14.

Oh! how I love, on a fair summer's eve,
When streams of light pour down the golden west,
And on the balmy zephyrs tranquil rest
The silver clouds, far—far away to leave
All meaner thoughts, and take a sweet reprieve
From little cares; to find, with easy quest,
A fragrant wild, with Nature's beauty drest,
And there into delight my soul deceive.
There warm my breast with patriotic lore,
Musing on Milton's fate—on Sydney's bier—
Till their stern forms before my mind arise:
Perhaps on wing of Poesy upsoar,
Full often dropping a delicious tear,
When some melodious sorrow spells mine eyes.

July, 1816

15. TO MY BROTHER GEORGE

Many the wonders I this day have seen:
The sun, when first he kist away the tears
That fill'd the eyes of morn;—the laurell'd peers
Who from the feathery gold of evening lean;—
The ocean with its vastness, its blue green,
Its ships, its rocks, its caves, its hopes, its fears,—
Its voice mysterious, which whoso hears
Must think on what will be, and what has been.
E'en now, dear George, while this for you I write,
Cynthia is from her silken curtains peeping
So scantly, that it seems her bridal night,
And she her half-discover'd revels keeping.
But what, without the social thought of thee,
Would be the wonders of the sky and sea?

August, 1816

16. ON FIRST LOOKING INTO CHAPMAN'S HOMER

Much have I travell'd in the realms of gold,
And many goodly states and kingdoms seen;
Round many western islands have I been
Which bards in fealty to Apollo hold.
Oft of one wide expanse had I been told
That deep-brow'd Homer ruled as his demesne;
Yet did I never breathe its pure serene
Till I heard Chapman speak out loud and bold:
Then felt I like some watcher of the skies
When a new planet swims into his ken;
Or like stout Cortez when with eagle eyes
He star'd at the Pacific—and all his men
Look'd at each other with a wild surmise—
Silent, upon a peak in Darien.

October, 1816

17.

Keen, fitful gusts are whisp'ring here and there
Among the bushes half leafless, and dry;
The stars look very cold about the sky,
And I have many miles on foot to fare.
Yet feel I little of the cool bleak air,
Or of the dead leaves rustling drearily,
Or of those silver lamps that burn on high,
Or of the distance from home's pleasant lair:
For I am brimful of the friendliness
That in a little cottage I have found;
Of fair-hair'd Milton's eloquent distress,
And all his love for gentle Lycid drown'd;
Of lovely Laura in her light green dress,
And faithful Petrarch gloriously crown'd.

Early November, 1816

18.   TO HAYDON

Highmindedness, a jealousy for good,
A loving-kindness for the great man's fame,
Dwells here and there with people of no name,
In noisome alley, and in pathless wood:
And where we think the truth least understood,
Oft may be found a 'singleness of aim,'
That ought to frighten into hooded shame
A money-mong'ring, pitiable brood.
How glorious this affection for the cause
Of stedfast genius, toiling gallantly!
What when a stout unbending champion awes
Envy, and Malice to their native sty?
Unnumber'd souls breathe out a still applause,
Proud to behold him in his country's eye.

Early November, 1816

19. TO A LADY WHO SENT ME A LAUREL CROWN

Fresh morning gusts have blown away all fear
From my glad bosom,—now from gloominess
I mount forever—not an atom less
Than the proud laurel shall content my bier.
No! by the eternal stars! or why sit here
In the Sun's eye, and 'gainst my temples press
Apollo's very leaves, woven to bless
By thy white fingers and thy spirit clear.
Lo! who dares say, "Do this"? Who dares call down
My will from its high purpose? Who say, "Stand,"
Or "Go"? This mighty moment I would frown
On abject Caesars—not the stoutest band
Of mailed heroes should tear off my crown:
Yet would I kneel and kiss thy gentle hand.

November, 1816

20. TO MY BROTHERS

Small, busy flames play through the fresh laid coals,
And their faint cracklings o'er our silence creep
Like whispers of the household gods that keep
A gentle empire o'er fraternal souls.
And while, for rhymes, I search around the poles,
Your eyes are fix'd, as in poetic sleep,
Upon the lore so voluble and deep,
That aye at fall of night our care condoles.
This is your birth-day Tom, and I rejoice
That thus it passes smoothly, quietly.
Many such eves of gently whisp'ring noise
May we together pass, and calmly try
What are this world's true joys,—ere the great voice,
From its fair face, shall bid our spirits fly.

November 18, 1816

21. TO HAYDON

Great spirits now on earth are sojourning;
He of the cloud, the cataract, the lake,
Who on Helvellyn's summit, wide awake,
Catches his freshness from Archangel's wing:
He of the rose, the violet, the spring,
The social smile, the chain for Freedom's sake:
And lo!—whose stedfastness would never take
A meaner sound than Raphael's whispering.
And other spirits there are standing apart
Upon the forehead of the age to come;
These, these will give the world another heart,
And other pulses. Hear ye not the hum
Of mighty workings?—
Listen awhile ye nations, and be dumb.

November 19, 1816

22.

Before he went to feed with owls and bats
Nebuchadnezzar had an ugly dream,
Worse than an Hus'if's when she thinks her cream
Made a Naumachia for mice and rats.
So scared, he sent for that "Good King of Cats"
Young Daniel, who soon did pluck away the beam
From out his eye, and said he did not deem
The sceptre worth a straw—his Cushions old door-mats.
A horrid nightmare similar somewhat
Of late has haunted a most motley crew,
Most loggerheads and Chapmen—we are told
That any Daniel tho' he be a sot
Can make the lying lips turn pale of hue
By belching out "ye are that head of Gold."

November, 1816

23. ON LEAVING SOME FRIENDS AT AN EARLY HOUR

Give me a golden pen, and let me lean
On heap'd up flowers, in regions clear, and far;
Bring me a tablet whiter than a star,
Or hand of hymning angel, when 'tis seen
The silver strings of heavenly harp atween:
And let there glide by many a pearly car,
Pink robes, and wavy hair, and diamond jar,
And half discovered wings, and glances keen.
The while let music wander round my ears,
And as it reaches each delicious ending,
Let me write down a line of glorious tone,
And full of many wonders of the spheres:
For what a height my spirit is contending!
'Tis not content so soon to be alone.

November, 1816

24. TO G. A. W. [GEORGIANA AUGUSTA WYLIE]

Nymph of the downward smile and sidelong glance,
In what diviner moments of the day
Art thou most lovely?—when gone far astray
Into the labyrinths of sweet utterance,
Or when serenely wand'ring in a trance
Of sober thought?—or when starting away
With careless robe to meet the morning ray
Thou spar'st the flowers in thy mazy dance?
Haply 'tis when thy ruby lips part sweetly,
And so remain, because thou listenest:
But thou to please wert nurtured so completely
That I can never tell what mood is best.
I shall as soon pronounce which Grace more neatly
Trips it before Apollo than the rest.

December, 1816

25. TO KOSCIUSKO

Good Kosciusko, thy great name alone
Is a full harvest whence to reap high feeling;
It comes upon us like the glorious pealing
Of the wide spheres—an everlasting tone.
And now it tells me, that in worlds unknown,
The names of heroes, burst from the clouds concealing,
And change to harmonies, for ever stealing
Through cloudless blue, and round each silver throne.
It tells me too, that on a happy day,
When some good spirit walks upon the earth,
Thy name with Alfred's, and the great of yore
Gently commingling, gives tremendous birth
To a loud hymn, that sounds far, far away
To where the great God lives for evermore.

December, 1816

26.

Happy is England! I could be content
To see no other verdure than its own;
To feel no other breezes than are blown
Through its tall woods with high romances blent:
Yet do I sometimes feel a languishment
For skies Italian, and an inward groan
To sit upon an Alp as on a throne,
And half forget what world or worldling meant.
Happy is England, sweet her artless daughters;
Enough their simple loveliness for me,
Enough their whitest arms in silence clinging:
Yet do I often warmly burn to see
Beauties of deeper glance, and hear their singing,
And float with them about the summer waters.

December, 1816

27.   THE POET

At Morn, at Noon, at Eve, and Middle Night,
He passes forth into the charmed air,
With talisman to call up spirits rare
From plant, cave, rock, and fountain.—To his sight
The hush of natural objects opens quite
To the core: and every secret essence there
Reveals the elements of good and fair;
Making him see, where Learning hath no light.
Sometimes, above the gross and palpable things
Of this diurnal ball, his spirit flies
On awful wing; and with its destined skies
Holds premature and mystic communings:
Till such unearthly intercourses shed
A visible halo round his mortal head.

December, 1816

28.   WRITTEN IN DISGUST OF VULGAR SUPERSTITION

The church bells toll a melancholy round,
Calling the people to some other prayers,
Some other gloominess, more dreadful cares,
More hearkening to the sermon's horrid sound.
Surely the mind of man is closely bound
In some black spell; seeing that each one tears
Himself from fireside joys, and Lydian airs,
And converse high of those with glory crown'd.
Still, still they toll, and I should feel a damp,—
A chill as from a tomb, did I not know
That they are dying like an outburnt lamp;
That 'tis their sighing, wailing ere they go
Into oblivion;—that fresh flowers will grow,
And many glories of immortal stamp.

December 22, 1816

29. ON THE GRASSHOPPER AND CRICKET

The poetry of earth is never dead:
When all the birds are faint with the hot sun,
And hide in cooling trees, a voice will run
From hedge to hedge about the new-mown mead;
That is the Grasshopper's—he takes the lead
In summer luxury,—he has never done
With his delights; for when tired out with fun
He rests at ease beneath some pleasant weed.
The poetry of earth is ceasing never:
On a lone winter evening, when the frost
Has wrought a silence, from the stove there shrills
The Cricket's song, in warmth increasing ever,
And seems to one in drowsiness half lost,
The Grasshopper's among some grassy hills.

December 30, 1816

30.

After dark vapors have oppress'd our plains
For a long dreary season, comes a day
Born of the gentle South, and clears away
From the sick heavens all unseemly stains.
The anxious month, relieved of its pains,
Takes as a long-lost right the feel of May;
The eyelids with the passing coolness play
Like rose leaves with the drip of Summer rains.
The calmest thoughts come round us; as of leaves
Budding—fruit ripening in stillness—Autumn suns
Smiling at eve upon the quiet sheaves—
Sweet Sappho's cheek—a smiling infant's breath—
The gradual sand that through an hour-glass runs—
A woodland rivulet—a Poet's death.

January 31, 1817

31. ON RECEIVING A LAUREL CROWN
FROM LEIGH HUNT

Minutes are flying swiftly, and as yet
Nothing unearthly has enticed my brain
Into a delphic Labyrinth—I would fain
Catch an unmortal thought to pay the debt
I owe to the kind Poet who has set
Upon my ambitious head a glorious gain.
Two bending laurel Sprigs—'tis nearly pain
To be conscious of such a Coronet.
Still time is fleeting, and no dream arises
Gorgeous as I would have it—only I see
A Trampling down of what the world most prizes
Turbans and Crowns, and blank regality;
And then I run into most wild surmises
Of all the many glories that may be.

February, 1817

32. TO THE LADIES WHO SAW ME CROWN'D

What is there in the universal Earth
More lovely than a Wreath from the bay tree?
Haply a Halo round the Moon—a glee
Circling from three sweet pair of Lips in Mirth;
And haply you will say the dewy birth
Of morning Roses—riplings tenderly
Spread by the Halcyon's breast upon the Sea—
But these Comparisons are nothing worth—
Then is there nothing in the world so fair?
The silvery tears of April?—Youth of May?
Or June that breathes out life for butterflies?
No—none of these can from my favourite bear
Away the Palm—yet shall it ever pay
Due Reverence to your most sovereign eyes.

February, 1817

33. TO LEIGH HUNT, ESQ.

Glory and loveliness have pass'd away;
For if we wander out in early morn,
No wreathed incense do we see upborne
Into the east, to meet the smiling day:
No crowd of nymphs soft voic'd, and young, and gay,
In woven baskets bringing ears of corn,
Roses, and pinks, and violets, to adorn
The shrine of Flora in her early May.
But there are left delights as high as these,
And I shall ever bless my destiny,
That in a time, when under pleasant trees
Pan is no longer sought, I feel a free,
A leafy luxury, seeing I could please
With these poor offerings, a man like thee.

Middle of February, 1817

34. WRITTEN AT THE END OF "THE FLOURE
AND THE LEFE"

This pleasant tale is like a little copse:
The honied lines do freshly interlace
To keep the reader in so sweet a place,
So that he here and there full-hearted stops;
And oftentimes he feels the dewy drops
Come cool and suddenly against his face,
And by the wandering melody may trace
Which way the tender-legged linnet hops.
Oh! what a power hath white Simplicity!
What mighty power has this gentle story!
I that for ever feel athirst for glory
Could at this moment be content to lie
Meekly upon the grass, as those whose sobbings
Were heard of none beside the mournful robins.

February [26?], 1817

35. ON SEEING THE ELGIN MARBLES

My spirit is too weak—mortality
Weighs heavily on me like unwilling sleep,
And each imagin'd pinnacle and steep
Of godlike hardship, tells me I must die
Like a sick Eagle looking at the sky.
Yet 'tis a gentle luxury to weep
That I have not the cloudy winds to keep,
Fresh for the opening of the morning's eye.
Such dim-conceived glories of the brain
Bring round the heart an undescribable feud;
So do these wonders a most dizzy pain,
That mingles Grecian grandeur with the rude
Wasting of old Time—with a billowy main—
A sun—a shadow of a magnitude.

March 1 or 3, 1817

36. TO HAYDON, WITH A SONNET WRITTEN ON SEEING THE ELGIN MARBLES

Haydon! forgive me that I cannot speak
Definitely on these mighty things;
Forgive me that I have not Eagle's wings—
That what I want I know not where to seek:
And think that I would not be over meek
In rolling out upfollow'd thunderings,
Even to the steep of Heliconian springs,
Were I of ample strength for such a freak—
Think too, that all those numbers should be thine;
Whose else? In this who touch thy vesture's hem?
For when men star'd at what was most divine
With browless idiotism—o'erwise phlegm—
Thou hadst beheld the Hesperean shine
Of their star in the East, and gone to worship them.

March 1 or 3, 1817

37. ON A PICTURE OF LEANDER

Come hither all sweet maidens soberly,
Down-looking aye, and with a chasten'd light,
Hid in the fringes of your eyelids white,
And meekly let your fair hands joined be,
As if so gentle that ye could not see,
Untouch'd, a victim of your beauty bright,
Sinking away to his young spirit's night,—
Sinking bewilder'd 'mid the dreary sea:
'Tis young Leander toiling to his death;
Nigh swooning, he doth purse his weary lips
For Hero's cheek, and smiles against her smile.
O horrid dream! see how his body dips
Dead-heavy; arms and shoulders gleam awhile:
He's gone; up bubbles all his amorous breath!

March, 1817

38. ON LEIGH HUNT'S POEM "THE STORY OF RIMINI"

Who loves to peer up at the morning sun,
With half-shut eyes and comfortable cheek,
Let him, with this sweet tale, full often seek
For meadows where the little rivers run;
Who loves to linger with that brightest one
Of Heaven—Hesperus—let him lowly speak
These numbers to the night, and starlight meek,
Or moon, if that her hunting be begun.
He who knows these delights, and too is prone
To moralize upon a smile or tear,
Will find at once a region of his own,
A bower for his spirit, and will steer
To alleys where the fir-tree drops its cone,
Where robins hop, and fallen leaves are sear.

March, 1817

39. ON THE SEA

It keeps eternal whisperings around
Desolate shores, and with its mighty swell
Gluts twice ten thousand Caverns, till the spell
Of Hecate leaves them their old shadowy sound.
Often 'tis in such gentle temper found,
That scarcely will the very smallest shell
Be mov'd for days from where it sometime fell,
When last the winds of Heaven were unbound.
Oh ye! who have your eye-balls vex'd and tir'd,
Feast them upon the wideness of the Sea;
Oh ye! whose ears are dinn'd with uproar rude,
Or fed too much with cloying melody—
Sit ye near some old Cavern's Mouth, and brood
Until ye start, as if the sea-nymphs quir'd.

April 17, 1817

40. TO A CAT

Cat! who hast pass'd thy grand climacteric,
How many mice and rats hast in thy days
Destroy'd?—How many tit bits stolen? Gaze
With those bright languid segments green, and prick
Those velvet ears—but pr'ythee do not stick
Thy latent talons in me—and upraise
Thy gentle mew—and tell me all thy frays
Of fish and mice, and rats and tender chick.
Nay, look not down, nor lick thy dainty wrists—
For all the wheezy asthma,—and for all
Thy tail's tip is nick'd off—and though the fists
Of many a maid have given thee many a maul,
Still is that fur as soft as when the lists
In youth thou enter'dst on glass bottled wall.

January 16, 1818

41. ON SITTING DOWN TO READ KING LEAR ONCE AGAIN

O golden tongued Romance, with serene lute!
Fair plumed Syren, Queen of far-away!
Leave melodizing on this wintry day,
Shut up thine olden pages, and be mute:
Adieu! for, once again, the fierce dispute
Betwixt damnation and impassion'd clay
Must I burn through; once more humbly assay
The bitter-sweet of this Shakespearian fruit:
Chief Poet! and ye clouds of Albion,
Begetters of our deep eternal theme!
When through the old oak Forest I am gone,
Let me not wander in a barren dream,
But, when I am consumed in the fire,
Give me new Phoenix wings to fly at my desire.

January 22, 1818

42.

When I have fears that I may cease to be
Before my pen has glean'd my teeming brain,
Before high-piled books, in charactery,
Hold like rich garners the full ripen'd grain;
When I behold, upon the night's starr'd face,
Huge cloudy symbols of a high romance,
And think that I may never live to trace
Their shadows, with the magic hand of chance;
And when I feel, fair creature of an hour,
That I shall never look upon thee more,
Never have relish in the faery power
Of unreflecting love;—then on the shore
Of the wide world I stand alone, and think
Till love and fame to nothingness do sink.

January 22-31, 1818

43. TO A LADY SEEN FOR A FEW MOMENTS
AT VAUXHALL

Time's sea hath been five years at its slow ebb,
Long hours have to and fro let creep the sand,
Since I was tangled in thy beauty's web,
And snared by the ungloving of thine hand.
And yet I never look on midnight sky,
But I behold thine eyes' well memory'd light;
I cannot look upon the rose's dye,
But to thy cheek my soul doth take its flight.
I cannot look on any budding flower,
But my fond ear, in fancy at thy lips
And hearkening for a love-sound, doth devour
Its sweets in the wrong sense:—Thou dost eclipse
Every delight with sweet remembering,
And grief unto my darling joys dost bring.

February 4, 1818

44. TO THE NILE

Son of the old moon-mountains African!
Chief of the Pyramid and Crocodile!
We call thee fruitful, and, that very while,
A desert fills our seeing's inward span;
Nurse of swart nations since the world began,
Art thou so fruitful? or dost thou beguile
Such men to honor thee, who, worn with toil,
Rest for a space 'twixt Cairo and Decan?
O may dark fancies err! they surely do;
'Tis ignorance that makes a barren waste
Of all beyond itself, thou dost bedew
Green rushes like our rivers, and dost taste
The pleasant sun-rise, green isles hast thou too,
And to the sea as happily dost haste.

February 4, 1818

45.   TO SPENSER

Spenser! a jealous honourer of thine,
A forester deep in thy midmost trees,
Did last eve ask my promise to refine
Some English that might strive thine ear to please.
But Elfin Poet 'tis impossible
For an inhabitant of wintry earth
To rise like Phoebus with a golden quell
Fire-wing'd and make a morning in his mirth.
It is impossible to escape from toil
O' the sudden and receive thy spiriting:
The flower must drink the nature of the soil
Before it can put forth its blossoming:
Be with me in the summer days and I
Will for thine honour and his pleasure try.

February 5, 1818

46.   WRITTEN IN ANSWER TO A SONNET
ENDING THUS:—
Dark eyes are dearer far
Than those that mock the hyacinthine bell—
By J. H. Reynolds.

Blue! 'Tis the life of heaven,—the domain
Of Cynthia,—the wide palace of the sun,—
The tent of Hesperus, and all his train,—
The bosomer of clouds, gold, grey and dun.
Blue! 'Tis the life of waters:—Ocean
And all its vassal streams, pools numberless,
May rage, and foam, and fret, but never can
Subside, if not to dark blue nativeness.
Blue! Gentle cousin of the forest-green,
Married to green in all the sweetest flowers,—
Forget-me-not,—the Blue bell,—and, that Queen
Of secrecy, the Violet: what strange powers
Hast thou, as a mere shadow! But how great,
When in an Eye thou art, alive with fate!

February 8, 1818

47. WHAT THE THRUSH SAID

O thou whose face hath felt the Winter's wind,
Whose eye has seen the snow-clouds hung in mist,
And the black elm tops 'mong the freezing stars,
To thee the spring will be a harvest-time.
O thou, whose only book has been the light
Of supreme darkness which thou feddest on
Night after night when Phoebus was away,
To thee the Spring shall be a triple morn.
O fret not after knowledge—I have none,
And yet my song comes native with the warmth.
O fret not after knowledge—I have none,
And yet the Evening listens. He who saddens
At thought of idleness cannot be idle,
And he's awake who thinks himself asleep.

February 19, 1818

48. THE HUMAN SEASONS

Four seasons fill the measure of the year;
There are four seasons in the mind of man:
He has his lusty Spring, when fancy clear
Takes in all beauty with an easy span:
He has his Summer, when luxuriously
Spring's honied cud of youthful thought he loves
To ruminate, and by such dreaming nigh
His nearest unto heaven: quiet coves
His soul has in its Autumn, when his wings
He furleth close; contented so to look
On mists in idleness—to let fair things
Pass by unheeded as a threshold brook.
He has his Winter too of pale misfeature,
Or else he would forego his mortal nature.

March 13, 1818

49.   TO JOHN HAMILTON REYNOLDS

O that a week could be an age, and we
Felt parting and warm meeting every week,
Then one poor year a thousand years would be,
The flush of welcome ever on the cheek:
So could we live long life in little space,
So time itself would be annihilate,
So a day's journey in oblivious haze
To serve our joys would lengthen and dilate.
O to arrive each Monday morn from Ind!
To land each Tuesday from the rich Levant!
In little time a host of joys to bind,
And keep our souls in one eternal pant!
This morn, my friend, and yester-evening taught
Me how to harbour such a happy thought.

April 20 or 21, 1818

50.   TO HOMER

Standing aloof in giant ignorance,
Of thee I hear and of the Cyclades,
As one who sits ashore and longs perchance
To visit dolphin-coral in deep seas.
So thou wast blind;—but then the veil was rent,
For Jove uncurtain'd Heaven to let thee live,
And Neptune made for thee a spumy tent,
And Pan made sing for thee his forest-hive;
Aye on the shores of darkness there is light,
And precipices show untrodden green,
There is a budding morrow in midnight,
There is a triple sight in blindness keen;
Such seeing hadst thou, as it once befell
To Dian, Queen of Earth, and Heaven, and Hell.

About April 27, 1818

51. ON VISITING THE TOMB OF BURNS

The town, the churchyard, and the setting sun,
The clouds, the trees, the rounded hills all seem,
Though beautiful, cold—strange—as in a dream,
I dreamed long ago, now new begun.
The short-liv'd, paly Summer is but won
From Winter's ague, for one hour's gleam;
Though sapphire-warm, their stars do never beam:
All is cold Beauty; pain is never done:
For who has mind to relish, Minos-wise,
The Real of Beauty, free from that dead hue
Sickly imagination and sick pride
Cast wan upon it! Burns! with honour due
I oft have honour'd thee. Great shadow, hide
Thy face; I sin against thy native skies.

July 1, 1818

52. TO AILSA ROCK

Hearken, thou craggy ocean pyramid!
Give answer from thy voice, the sea-fowls' screams!
When were thy shoulders mantled in huge streams?
When, from the sun, was thy broad forehead hid?
How long is't since the mighty power bid
Thee heave to airy sleep from fathom dreams?
Sleep in the lap of thunder or sunbeams,
Or when grey clouds are thy cold coverlid.
Thou answer'st not; for thou art dead asleep;
Thy life is but two dead eternities—
The last in air, the former in the deep;
First with the whales, last with the eagle-skies—
Drown'd wast thou till an earthquake made thee steep,
Another cannot wake thy giant size.

July 10, 1818

53. WRITTEN IN THE COTTAGE WHERE BURNS WAS BORN

This mortal body of a thousand days
Now fills, O Burns, a space in thine own room,
Where thou didst dream alone on budded bays,
Happy and thoughtless of thy day of doom!
My pulse is warm with thine own Barley-bree,
My head is light with pledging a great soul,
My eyes are wandering, and I cannot see,
Fancy is dead and drunken at its goal;
Yet can I stamp my foot upon thy floor,
Yet can I ope thy window-sash to find
The meadow thou hast tramped o'er and o'er,—
Yet can I think of thee till thought is blind,—
Yet can I gulp a bumper to thy name,—
O smile among the shades, for this is fame!

July 11, 1818

54. ON HEARING THE BAG-PIPE AND SEEING "THE STRANGER" PLAYED AT INVERARY

Of late two dainties were before me plac'd
Sweet, holy, pure, sacred and innocent,
From the ninth sphere to me benignly sent
That Gods might know my own particular taste:
First the soft Bag-pipe mourn'd with zealous haste,
The Stranger next with head on bosom bent
Sigh'd; rueful again the piteous Bag-pipe went,
Again the Stranger sighings fresh did waste.
O Bag-pipe thou didst steal my heart away—
A Stranger thou my nerves from Pipe didst charm—
O Bag-pipe thou didst re-assert thy sway—
Again thou Stranger gav'st me fresh alarm—
Alas! I could not choose. Ah! my poor heart,
Mum chance art thou with both oblig'd to part.

July 18, 1818

55.   WRITTEN ON THE TOP OF BEN NEVIS

Read me a lesson, Muse, and speak it loud
Upon the top of Nevis, blind in mist!
I look into the chasms, and a shroud
Vaporous doth hide them,—just so much I wist
Mankind do know of hell; I look o'erhead,
And there is sullen mist,—even so much
Mankind can tell of heaven; mist is spread
Before the earth, beneath me,—even such,
Even so vague is man's sight of himself!
Here are the craggy stones beneath my feet,—
Thus much I know that, a poor witless elf,
I tread on them,—that all my eye doth meet
Is mist and crag, not only on this height,
But in the world of thought and mental might!

August 2, 1818

56.   TRANSLATION FROM A SONNET OF RONSARD

Nature withheld Cassandra in the skies,
For more adornment, a full thousand years;
She took their cream of Beauty's fairest dyes,
And shap'd and tinted her above all Peers:
Meanwhile Love kept her dearly with his wings,
And underneath their shadow fill'd her eyes
With such a richness that the cloudy Kings
Of high Olympus utter'd slavish sighs.
When from the Heavens I saw her first descend,
My heart took fire, and only burning pains,
They were my pleasures—they my Life's sad end;
Love pour'd her beauty into my warm veins . . .
*   *   *   *   *   *   *
*   *   *   *   *   *   *

September 21, 1818

57.

Why did I laugh tonight? No voice will tell:
No God, no Demon of severe response,
Deigns to reply from heaven or from Hell.
Then to my human heart I turn at once.
Heart! Thou and I are here sad and alone;
I say, why did I laugh! O mortal pain!
O Darkness! Darkness! ever must I moan,
To question Heaven and Hell and Heart in vain.
Why did I laugh? I know this Being's lease,
My fancy to its utmost blisses spreads;
Yet would I on this very midnight cease,
And the world's gaudy ensigns see in shreds;
Verse, Fame, and Beauty are intense indeed,
But Death intenser—Death is Life's high meed.

March, 1819

58.   A DREAM, AFTER READING DANTE'S EPISODE
OF PAOLO AND FRANCESCA

As Hermes once took to his feathers light,
When lulled Argus, baffled, swoon'd and slept,
So on a Delphic reed, my idle spright
So play'd, so charm'd, so conquer'd, so bereft
The dragon-world of all its hundred eyes;
And, seeing it asleep, so fled away—
Not to pure Ida with its snow-cold skies,
Nor unto Tempe where Jove griev'd a day;
But to that second circle of sad hell,
Where 'mid the gust, the whirlwind, and the flaw
Of rain and hail-stones, lovers need not tell
Their sorrows. Pale were the sweet lips I saw,
Pale were the lips I kiss'd, and fair the form
I floated with, about that melancholy storm.

April, 1819

59.

Bright star, would I were stedfast as thou art—
Not in lone splendour hung aloft the night
And watching, with eternal lids apart,
Like nature's patient, sleepless Eremite,
The moving waters at their priestlike task
Of pure ablution round earth's human shores,
Or gazing on the new soft-fallen mask
Of snow upon the mountains and the moors—
No—yet still stedfast, still unchangeable,
Pillow'd upon my fair love's ripening breast,
To feel for ever its soft fall and swell,
Awake for ever in a sweet unrest,
Still, still to hear her tender-taken breath,
And so live ever—or else swoon to death.

April, 1819

60. TO SLEEP

O soft embalmer of the still midnight,
Shutting, with careful fingers and benign,
Our gloom-pleas'd eyes, embower'd from the light,
Enshaded in forgetfulness divine:
O soothest Sleep! if so it please thee, close
In midst of this thine hymn my willing eyes,
Or wait the "Amen," ere thy poppy throws
Around my bed its lulling charities.
Then save me, or the passed day will shine
Upon my pillow, breeding many woes,—
Save me from curious Conscience, that still lords
Its strength for darkness, burrowing like a mole;
Turn the key deftly in the oiled wards,
And seal the hushed Casket of my Soul.

April, 1819

61. ON FAME

Fame, like a wayward Girl, will still be coy
To those who woo her with too slavish knees,
But makes surrender to some thoughtless Boy,
And dotes the more upon a heart at ease;
She is a Gipsey, will not speak to those
Who have not learnt to be content without her;
A Jilt, whose ear was never whisper'd close,
Who thinks they scandal her who talk about her;
A very Gipsey is she, Nilus-born,
Sister-in-law to jealous Potiphar;
Ye love-sick Bards, repay her scorn for scorn,
Ye Artists lovelorn, madmen that ye are!
Make your best bow to her and bid adieu,
Then, if she likes it, she will follow you.

April 30, 1819

62. ON THE SAME

"You cannot eat your cake and have it too."—*Proverb*

How fever'd is the man, who cannot look
Upon his mortal days with temperate blood,
Who vexes all the leaves of his life's book,
And robs his fair name of its maidenhood;
It is as if the rose should pluck herself,
Or the ripe plum finger its misty bloom,
As if a Naiad, like a meddling elf,
Should darken her pure grot with muddy gloom,
But the rose leaves herself upon the briar,
For winds to kiss and grateful bees to feed,
And the ripe plum still wears its dim attire,
The undisturbed lake has crystal space,
Why then should man, teasing the world for grace,
Spoil his salvation for a fierce miscreed?

April 30, 1819

63. ON THE SONNET

If by dull rhymes our English must be chain'd,
And, like Andromeda, the Sonnet sweet
Fetter'd, in spite of pained loveliness,
Let us find out, if we must be constrain'd,
Sandals more interwoven and complete
To fit the naked foot of Poesy:
Let us inspect the Lyre, and weigh the stress
Of every chord, and see what may be gain'd
By ear industrious, and attention meet;
Misers of sound and syllable, no less
Than Midas of his coinage, let us be
Jealous of dead leaves in the bay wreath crown;
So, if we may not let the Muse be free,
She will be bound with garlands of her own.

April, 1819

64.

The House of Mourning written by Mr. Scott,—
A sermon at the Magdalen,—A tear
Dropt on a greasy novel,—Want of cheer
After a walk up hill to a friend's cot,—
Tea with a maiden Lady—A curs'd lot
Of worthy poems with the Author near,—
A patron lord—A drunkenness from beer,—
Haydon's great picture,—A cold coffee pot
At midnight, when the Muse is ripe for labour,—
The voice of Mr. Coleridge,—A french Bonnet,—
Before you in the pit,—A pipe & tabour,—
A damn'd inseparable flute and neighbor,—
All these are vile,—But viler Wordsworth's sonnet
On Dover:—Dover!—Who *could* write upon it?

June, 1819

65.

The day is gone, and all its sweets are gone!
Sweet voice, sweet lips, soft hand, and softer breast,
Warm breath, light whisper, tender semi-tone,
Bright eyes, accomplish'd shape, and lang'rous waist!
Faded the flower and all its budded charms,
Faded the sight of beauty from my eyes,
Faded the shape of beauty from my arms,
Faded the voice, warmth, whiteness, paradise—
Vanish'd unseasonably at shut of eve,
When the dusk holiday—or holinight
Of fragrant-curtain'd love begins to weave
The woof of darkness thick, for hid delight;
But, as I've read love's missal through to-day,
He'll let me sleep, seeing I fast and pray.

October 10, 1819

66. TO FANNY

I cry your mercy—pity—love!—aye, love!
Merciful love that tantalizes not,
One-thoughted, never-wandering, guileless love,
Unmask'd, and being seen—without a blot!
O! let me have thee whole,—all—all—be mine!
That shape, that fairness, that sweet minor zest
Of love, your kiss,—those hands, those eyes divine,
That warm, white, lucent, million-pleasured breast,—
Yourself—your soul—in pity give me all,
Withhold no atom's atom or I die,
Or living on perhaps, your wretched thrall,
Forget, in the mist of idle misery,
Life's purposes,—the palate of my mind
Losing its gust, and my ambition blind!

November or December, 1819

67.   TO A. G. S. [AUBREY GEORGE SPENCER]

Where didst thou find, young Bard, thy sounding lyre?
Where the bland accent, & the tender tone?
A-sitting snugly by the Parlour fire;
Or didst thou with Apollo pick a bone?
The Muse will have a crow to pick with me
For thus assaying in thy brightening path—
Who, that with his own brace of eyes can see,
Unthunderstruck beholds thy gentle wrath?
Who from a pot of stout e'er blew the froth
Into the bosom of the wandering wind,
Light as the Powder on the back of Moth,
But drank thy muses with a grateful mind.
Yea unto thee Beldams drink metheglin
And annisies, and carraway, and gin.

No date given

Appendix II:

Incidental Conclusions, Notes, Bibliography

APPENDIX II
INCIDENTAL CONCLUSIONS

In arriving at the conclusions for the sonnet versecraft of Keats through use of the comparative method, incidental evidence has thrown light on the sonnet craft of the other writers in the group, justifying a second body of conclusions. For Milton and Hunt, since all or a large part of their work was considered, the following sets of enumerated characteristics are reasonably complete; for the others, the representative sonnets studied are suggestive, but the necessity of selection makes the conclusions tentative. In addition to the characteristics of the writers, certain conclusions relating to the sonnet as a literary type are justified by the range in form and time (from Spenser to Keats) of the poems treated.

In determining conclusions for the poets, only those characteristics in which they differ from the average have been considered. To a large extent there will, of course, be general agreement between writers using the same form, and the points at which they differ will then be suggestive of the individual traits.

The Sonnet As a Literary Form

In the course of this study, detailed analyses have been made of 167 sonnets, containing a total of 2,336 verses. These have been chosen from the leading sonnet writers of a period covering two and a half centuries. From the comparative approach to this body of material have come the following conclusions relating to the sonnet as a literary form:

1. In the period involved (from Spenser to Keats), there was much experimentation and little legislation, with Leigh Hunt making the first important published contribution to the latter field some years after the death of Keats.

2. Out of the experiments and the attempt to adapt the form to the English language, there emerged three well-defined types of sonnet: the Italian, the Spenserian, and the Shakespearean. These were used with varying degrees of regularity by writers of the seventeenth and later centuries, following their introduction into the Elizabethan period. The Italian was most widely used, the Shakespearean second, and the Spenserian only infrequently.

3. Principal changes in the English use of the Italian form were Milton's abandonment of the strict octave pause, and his freer use of the heroic meter (both emulated by many eighteenth-century writers); and Wordsworth's admission of a third rime to the octave. All of these changes were justified by Italian precedent.

4. The historical development of the sonnet does not justify the dogmatic canons of modern purists, who would deny any creative freedom to an already rigid structure. Artistic principles leading to variety within uniformity must, and do, apply, and the sonnet is admirably adapted to both elements. The question of the closing couplet is one that cannot be decided by legislation, unless such legislation allows the decision to rest on appropriateness of relationship between form and content.

5. The range of sonnet themes had, by the time of Keats (and under the influence of Milton, Wordsworth, and their imitators), widened to include practically any subject; and themes were treated humorously as well as seriously.

6. The most widely used octave pattern in the Italian form was *abbaabba,* and two patterns dominated the sestet, *cdcdcd* and *cdecde.*

7. The Shakespearean and Spenserian forms almost invariably maintained their integrity of pattern.

8. Rimes approximate in sound were used consistently (as judged by available evidence of orthoëpy), probably as a result of the scarcity of exact rimes in English. Rimes approximate in accent were used more sparingly, since stronger verse endings resulted from avoidance of the type. Identical rimes were infrequent, but present in many writers.

9. Alliteration and assonance increased the effectiveness of variety within uniformity, and frequently (possibly unconsciously) emphasized unity of structure. Thus, beginnings of verses or phrases might be related to the close, or one verse bound more closely to another, through use of these effects. Carelessness in use of sound devices occasionally resulted in unfortunate and intrusive echoes within the verses.

10. Rhythmically there appeared, between the time of the Elizabethans and Keats, a gradually increasing flexibility in the use of heroic sonnet verse. This resulted from the inclusion of more variants, a freer distribution of caesurae and enjambment verses, and a generally greater freedom in phrasing.

11. On the evidence of the relationship between the sonnets and

the nonsonnet poetry of Keats and Hunt it seems clear that use of the more restricted form resulted generally in greater restraint and regularity.

12. The more regular verses were employed in lines seven and eight (regardless of the form used) and again at the close of the sonnet. This use conformed to the larger divisions of the sonnet and tended to strengthen the poem as a whole.

13. Variants occurred primarily in foot one, secondarily in foot three or four. There was thus a tendency to avoid putting two variants together in any large number of cases, as well as a tendency to permit the verse to end with a normal iambic.

14. The pyrrhic occurred most frequently in foot three, while the trochee is consistently used as a variant in foot one and the spondee most frequently either in foot one or two.

15. Only Shakespeare and Milton used the true pentameter invariably, the other writers admitting a wide range of non-pentameter verses, many of these being heroic tetrameters, of which the writers were probably not conscious.

16. End-stopped verses were more prevalent in the Elizabethan than in the later period.

17. End-stopping, regardless of the sonnet pattern, occurred most frequently at the close of verses four, eight, and twelve, suggesting a tendency to develop thought in quatrain units.

18. Enjambment was largely a matter of individual phrasing habits, with greater freedom among the later as compared with the Elizabethan writers.

19. Feminine and pyrrhic endings were not widely used, but there was a more consistent use of the latter.

20. Although a high degree of individuality was present in the use of medial pauses, the masculine type occurred in consistently larger numbers than those of the feminine type.

21. The heroic meter seemed to determine that approximately one fourth of all phrases would be of five-foot length, with the next larger frequencies, in order, in phrases of two-, three-, and one-foot length.

22. Extreme individuality was shown in the use of longer (noncomma) phrases, but in general when the phrase started at the verse opening it was two verses (or approximately ten feet) in length. The other lengths preferred were, in order, one, four, and three verses. When the phrase opened medially its normal

length was one and one-half verses, with one-half verse as second choice. When the phrase both opened and closed medially a length of one verse predominated.

23. The average relationship between phrases opening with unaccented or accented syllables was 65 per cent for the former and 35 for the latter.

24. The heroic meter was varied most frequently by four type groups of phrase variants, occurring at any point and not necessarily coinciding with the feet involved. The patterns determining these groups were, in order of importance, / x x /, x / x x x /, / / x /, and x / / /. A number of other patterns appeared in smaller numbers and with individual emphasis, but the foregoing were most frequently employed.

Hunt

The following conclusions seem justified for Hunt on the basis of an analysis of 392 verses. These represent all of the sonnets written before 1819 (all that might have influenced Keats), except those nontypical examples in the *Juvenilia*.

1. Hunt's was the primary influence on the sonnets of Keats.

2. His principal contribution to the sonnet as a type was the formulation of a detailed critical theory of the Italian pattern.

3. After an imitative and nontypical attempt in the Shakespearean form, in the *Juvenilia*, he turned to a rigid use and defense of the Italian.

4. Hunt maintained the most even balance of the group between the different types of rime.

5. He was the lowest of the group (though within 1 per cent of Keats) in the use of normal and approximately normal verses; and was high (equal with Keats) in his use of verses varied in three feet.

6. Like Keats, he showed more restraint in the sonnets than in the nonsonnet poetry.

7. His tendency was to open the sonnet with a fairly regular verse, and to re-emphasize regularity in verses four, seven, eight, eleven, and twelve. He was unusual in closing the sestet with relatively irregular verses.

8. He had only two occurrences of nonpentameter verses (both hexameters) in the sonnets considered.

9. Hunt was low in his use of end-stopped verses, but employed an end-stopped verse invariably at the close of the octave.

10. He was well balanced in his use of enjambment verses.

11. In the employment of feminine endings he was slightly higher than the others.

12. He used fewer caesurae than did Keats, but more comma pauses.

13. Hunt preferred the shorter (two-, three-, and four-feet) phrases, and was lowest in the group for phrases of five-foot length.

14. Of the longer (noncomma) phrases he preferred, in order, those of one-, four-, and one-half-verse lengths.

Bowles

140 verses from the sonnets of Bowles were analyzed. This is a number commensurate with his position in the development of the sonnet, and the poems chosen are thoroughly typical of his sonnet technique. Individual characteristics may be summarized as follows:

1. Bowles's contribution to the sonnet was largely one of subject matter—an influential extension of themes to include nature and places visited.

2. He was extreme in his use of rime types, being high in vowel echoes in nonintended rime words, and, based on Walker's *Dictionary,* low in his percentage of approximate rimes.

3. He was close to the Elizabethans in his use of approximately regular verses.

4. His tendency was to open the sonnet with a fairly regular verse, to re-emphasize the regularity at the close of the octave, and at the opening and close of the sestet.

5. Bowles had, like Wordsworth, a pronounced tendency to substitute a spondee in foot one.

6. He substituted a pyrrhic in foot two more frequently than did the others.

7. He had two nonpentameter verses (both hexameters) in the sonnets considered.

8. He was low in the number of end-stopped verses used, but was well balanced in his use of enjambment.

9. Bowles was unusual in having no occurrences of feminine ending, and he was low in percentage of pyrrhic ending.

10. In using medial pauses, he preferred the masculine comma type, having a high percentage of these.

11. Of the longer (noncomma) phrases he preferred, in order, those of two-, four-, one-, and three-verse lengths.

Wordsworth

210 representative verses were analyzed in the case of Wordsworth. From these the following characteristics have been determined:

1. Wordsworth's contributions to the form were an extension of Milton's freedom, use of the *abbaacca* octave, and the definite establishment of nature as a theme.

2. He seldom permitted vowel echoes in nonintended rimes.

3. His tendency was to open the sonnet with fairly irregular verses, establish regularity in verse five, and again at the opening and closing of the sestet.

4. He employed a high percentage of pyrrhics as variants, and, like Bowles, used the spondee frequently in the opening foot of the verse.

5. He had two heroic tetrameters in the sonnets considered.

6. Wordsworth was comparatively high in his use of end-stopped verses, and was well balanced in employment of the run-on line.

7. He was low in use of feminine endings, but slightly higher than the others in his use of pyrrhic endings.

8. He was nearest to Keats in the general frequency and use of medial pauses, and, like Keats, showed a preference for the feminine caesura.

9. Of the longer (noncomma) phrases, Wordsworth preferred, in order, those of one-, two-, and one-half-verse lengths.

Milton

For Milton, 252 verses (representing all of the fourteen-verse sonnets in English) were analyzed, leading to the following conclusions:

1. Milton's contributions to the form were a widening of the range of subject matter, a freer movement in the verse, and an irregular placement of the octave pause.

2. Judged by available evidence, he seldom used rimes approximate in accent.

3. His tendency was to open the sonnet with fairly irregular verses, to close the first quatrain and the octave with regularity, and to maintain the regular movement throughout the sestet.

4. All verses were true pentameters.

5. He used the fewest end-stopped verses of any in the group, with verse four having the main emphasis in this respect.

6. He made the freest use of enjambment verses.

7. Of the longer (noncomma) phrases he preferred, in order, those of two-, four-, and three-verse lengths.

8. Like Spenser and Shakespeare, he used slightly fewer phrase variants for each sonnet, indicating a regular movement.

Shakespeare

A study of 210 verses, representing sonnets from the entire range of his series, suggests the following conclusions as to Shakespeare's use of this form:

1. Shakespeare's contribution to the form was the establishment of the *abab cdcd efef gg* pattern.

2. Judged by available evidence, he was low in his use of rimes approximate in accent, and high in other types of rime.

3. His tendency was to open with a regular verse, to increase the regularity at the end of the second quatrain, to re-emphasize it in verse ten and especially in verse thirteen, and to close the sonnet with acceptable regularity.

4. All verses in the sonnets were true pentameters.

5. He had a high percentage of end-stopped verses, with an invariable pause at the end of verses four, eight, and twelve (based on available evidence as to punctuation). There was a tendency to pause also at the ends of verses two, six, and ten.

6. As a result of the foregoing, he was low in enjambment lines.

7. He was low in feminine caesurae, but high in masculine comma pauses.

8. Of the longer (noncomma) phrases he preferred, in order, those of two, one, and four verses, with a high percentage of those occupying two-verse lengths.

9. Like Milton and Spenser, he used slightly fewer phrase variants than did the others, indicating a regular movement.

Spenser

Fifteen sonnets (210 verses) from Spenser's "Amoretti" were analyzed. These represented the entire range of his sequence, and suggest the following conclusions:

1. Of the group considered, Spenser was by far the most metrically regular.

2. His principal contribution to the form was the establishment of the *abab bcbc cdcd ee* pattern, although he was also instrumental in introducing the Shakespearean sonnet.

3. He was highest in the group in his use of normal and approximately normal verses. These were well distributed, but emphasized at the close of the first and opening of the second quatrain, in verses seven and eight, strongly in verse ten, and acceptably at the sonnet close.

4. Whereas the other writers had the highest percentage of variation in foot one, with foot three next in importance, Spenser reversed the order.

5. He used comparatively few spondees and trochees as variants, but made habitual use of the pyrrhic in foot three.

6. Two hexameters and one heroic tetrameter occurred in the sonnets considered.

7. He was high in his use of end-stopped verses, with almost invariable occurrences at the ends of verses four, eight, and twelve; and a tendency to end-stop in verses two, six, and ten was exhibited.

8. He was very low in percentage of enjambment verses.

9. He was low in percentage of feminine endings.

10. He employed relatively few caesurae, the only occurrences being four parentheses.

11. He held with great rigidity to the five-foot phrase.

12. Of the longer (noncomma) phrases he preferred, in order, those of two- and four-verse lengths, with an extremely high percentage of the former.

13. He was high in percentage of phrases opening with unaccented syllables, and correspondingly low in those opening with an accent.

14. Like Milton and Shakespeare, he used slightly fewer phrase variants than did the others, indicating regular movement.

NOTES

The Oxford Edition of the poets has been taken as the basis for text with the following exceptions: Keats's sonnet, "The Poet" (number 27), first published by Amy Lowell, "The House of Mourning written by Mr. Scott" (number 64), first published by Claude Finney, and "To A.G.S." (number 67), first published by H. W. Garrod, are based on their printings. The sonnets of Bowles have been taken from various anthologies in the absence of an edition of his complete works.

PART ONE

1. Hunt, "Essay," p. 15.
2. Sharp, "The Sonnet," p. 22.
3. Figures, except for Keats and Hunt, from Hutchinson, "A Note on the Wordsworthian Sonnet," pp. 220-22.
4. Hutchinson, *loc. cit.*
5. Figures in Table II, except for Milton, Keats, and Hunt, from Hutchinson, *op. cit.*, pp. 225-26.
6. Crosland, *The English Sonnet*, p. 89, by permission of Dodd, Mead and Company, Inc.
7. *Op cit.*, p. 226.
8. *Op. cit.*, p. 15.
9. Smart, *The Sonnets of Milton*, pp. 17ff.
10. *Op. cit.*, p. 74.
11. Smart, *op. cit.*, p. 42.
12. *The Influence of Milton on English Poetry*, p. 482. All quotations from this work are by permission of Harvard University Press.
13. Paragraph on "The Verse" of "Paradise Lost."
14. *E.g.* by Mark Pattison, quoted in Smart, *op. cit.*, p. 28.
15. Smart, *op. cit.*, p. 31.
16. Havens, *op. cit.*, p. 488.
17. Table from Havens, *op. cit.*, p. 523.
18. All quotations based on Havens, *op. cit.*, chapter XIX.
19. *Ibid.*, p. 526.
20. Havens, *op. cit.*, pp. 487, 500.

21. *Ibid.*, p. 502.

22. Fenwick note in *Poetical Works*, ed. Knight, Vol. II, p. 323.

23. *Biographia Literaria*, p. 8.

24. Garrod, *Keats*, p. 146.

25. *Op. cit.*, pp. 21-22.

26. Undated letter of 1833 to Alexander Dyce, quoted in Havens, *op. cit.*, pp. 532-33.

27. *Op. cit.*, p. 218.

28. Letter 38. All letters from the M. B. Forman edition, by permission of Oxford University Press. Spelling and punctuation have been standardized. See p. 203 for identification.

29. Number 4.

30. *Lord Byron and ... Contemporaries*, Vol. I, pp. 409-10.

31. Blunden, *Leigh Hunt's Examiner Examined*, p. 69.

32. See sonnets numbers 4, 17, 21, 23, 29, 31, 32, 33, 38, 44.

33. Quoted in Miller, *Leigh Hunt's Relations with Byron, Shelley and Keats*, pp. 138ff. The sonnet is number 21.

34. *Ibid.*

35. *The Examiner* for December 1, 1816.

36. *Ibid.*, July, 1817.

37. Quoted in Lowell, *John Keats*, Vol. I, p. 180.

38. *Ibid.*

39. *The Examiner*, July 6 and 13, 1817; quoted in Blunden, *op. cit.*, p. 134.

40. *The Indicator*, August 2 and 9, 1820; quoted in Blunden, *op. cit.*, p. 157.

41. See letters numbers 8a, 13, 14, 20, 23, 26, 34, 38, 41, 93, 107, 114, 147, 211, 215, 220, and 221, for references to Hunt.

42. *Op. cit.*, pp. 59-60.

43. Clarke, "Recollections of Keats," p. 92.

44. Letter 114.

45. Letter 48.

46. Letter 28.

47. Letter 114.

48. Letter 107.

49. Letter 127.

50. See sonnet number 45.

51. Letter 37.

52. Letter 72.

53. Letter 114.

54. Blunden, *op. cit.*, p. 82.

55. *Ibid.*, pp. 131-32.

56. Quoted in the Forman edition of the letters, p. 117.

57. Hunt, *Lord Byron and . . . Contemporaries*, Vol. I, p. 418.

58. *Imagination and Fancy*, p. 287.

59. *Keats*, pp. 77-97.

60. "Notes on Professor Garrod's *Keats*." Certain of Mr. Bushnell's arguments are obviously weak, but need not be answered here, since we are concerned mainly with his conclusion.

61. *Keats' Craftsmanship*, p. 205.

62. *Op. cit.*, p. 540.

63. Letter 60.

64. Letter 140.

65. Letter 147.

66. See the *Poetical Works*, pp. 481-85.

67. *Keats*, pp. 145-46.

68. *Op. cit.*, pp. 540-41.

69. "Essay," p. 75.

PART TWO

1. Page 284.

2. Letter 114.

3. A. J. Ellis: *On Early English Pronunciation.*

4. Otto Jespersen, *A Modern English Grammar*, fourth edition, Heidelberg, 1928.

5. *Op. cit.*, "Introduction," p. 30.

6. See above, p. 56.

7. Wolff, *An Essay on Keats's Treatment of the Heroic Rhythm and Blank Verse.*

8. Wolff, *op. cit.*, p. 73.

9. *Op. cit.*, p. 73.

10. Paragraph on "The Verse" of "Paradise Lost."

11. Letter 31.

12. Letter 59.

SELECTED BIBLIOGRAPHY

BLUNDEN, EDMUND: *Leigh Hunt's Examiner Examined*. N. Y. and London, Harper, 1928.

BUSHNELL, NELSON SHERWIN: "Notes on Professor Garrod's *Keats*." *Modern Language Notes*, May, 1929, Vol. XLIV, pp. 287-96.

[CLARKE, CHARLES COWDEN]: "Recollections of Keats by an Old Schoolfellow." *Atlantic Monthly*, January, 1861, Vol. VII, pp. 86-100.

CROSLAND, T. W. H.: *The English Sonnet*. N. Y., Dodd, Mead, 1917.

ELLIS, A. J.: *On Early English Pronunciation*. In five parts. London, Dryden House, 1869-89.

FINNEY, CLAUDE LEE: *The Evolution of Keats's Poetry*. 2 vols. Cambridge, Harvard, 1936.

GARROD, H. W.: *Keats*. London, Oxford, 1926.

HAVENS, R. D.: *The Influence of Milton on English Poetry*. Cambridge, Harvard, 1922.

HUNT, LEIGH: "An Essay on the Cultivation, History, and Varieties of the Species of Poem Called the Sonnet," in Hunt and Lee: *The Book of the Sonnet, q. v.*

HUNT, LEIGH: *Imagination and Fancy*. London, Smith Elder, 1910.

HUNT, LEIGH: *Juvenilia*. London, J. Whiting, 1802.

HUNT, LEIGH: *Lord Byron and Some of His Contemporaries*. 2nd edition, 2 vols., London, Henry Colburn, 1828.

HUNT, LEIGH: *Poetical Works*, edited by H. S. Milford. London, Oxford, 1923.

HUNT, LEIGH: *Table Talk*. London, Smith Elder, 1858.

HUNT, LEIGH: "What is Poetry," in *Imagination and Fancy, q. v.*

HUNT, LEIGH, and LEE, S. ADAMS: *The Book of the Sonnet*. London, Sampson, Low, Son, and Marston, 1867.

HUTCHINSON, THOMAS: "A Note on the Wordsworthian Sonnet," in Wordsworth, William: *Poems in Two Volumes, q. v.*

KEATS, JOHN: *The Letters of John Keats,* edited by Maurice Buxton Forman, 2 vols., London, Oxford, 1931. Quotations have been made from the following letters as numbered and identified by Forman:

  6. To Benjamin Robert Haydon, November 20, 1816.
  8a. To Charles Cowden Clarke, March 26, 1817.
  13. To Leigh Hunt, May 10, 1817.
  14. To Benjamin Robert Haydon, May 10, 1817.
  20. To John Hamilton Reynolds, September 21, 1817.
  23. To Benjamin Bailey, October 8, 1817.
  26. To the same, November 5, 1817.
  28. To John Hamilton Reynolds, November 22, 1817.
  31. To George and Thomas Keats, January 5, 1818.
  34. To the same, January 13, 1818.
  37. To Benjamin Bailey, January 23, 1818.
  38. To George and Thomas Keats, January 23, 1818.
  41. To John Hamilton Reynolds, February 3, 1818.
  48. To John Taylor, February 27, 1818.
  50. To Benjamin Bailey, March 13, 1818.
  59. To John Taylor, April 24, 1818.
  60. To John Hamilton Reynolds, April 27, 1818.
  72. To the same, July 11, 1818.
  83. To the same, September 21 or 22, 1818.
  85. To James Augustus Hessey, October 9, 1818.
  88. To Richard Woodhouse, October 27, 1818.
  93. To George and Georgiana Keats, 1818-19.
  107. To Benjamin Robert Haydon, March 8, 1819.
  114. To George and Georgiana Keats, February 14, 1819.
  127. To Fanny Brawne, July 8, 1819.
  140. To John Taylor, September 5, 1819.
  147. To George and Georgiana Keats, September 17, 1819.
  211. To Fanny Keats, July 22, 1820.
  215. To the same, August 14, 1820.
  220. To Charles Brown, August, 1820.
  221. To Fanny Keats, August 23, 1820.

KEATS, JOHN: *The Poetical Works of John Keats,* edited by H. Buxton Forman. London, Oxford, 1926.

LOWELL, AMY: *John Keats:* 2 vols., Boston and N. Y., Houghton Mifflin, 1925.

MILLER, BARNETTE: *Leigh Hunt's Relations with Byron, Shelley, and Keats.* N. Y., Columbia, 1910.

RIDLEY, M. R.: *Keats' Craftsmanship*. London, Oxford, 1933.

SHARP, WILLIAM: "The Sonnet: Its Characteristics and History," in *Studies and Appreciations*, selected and arranged by Mrs. William Sharp. N. Y., Duffield, 1912.

SMART, JOHN S.: *The Sonnets of Milton*. Glasgow, Maclehose, Jackson, 1921.

SMITH, GREGORY: *Elizabethan Critical Essays*. 2 vols., London, Oxford, 1904.

STERNER, LEWIS G.: *The Sonnet in American Literature*. University of Pennsylvania, 1930.

WALKER, JOHN: *A Critical Pronouncing Dictionary and Expositor of the English Language*. Third edition, London, 1802.

WOLFF, LUCIEN: *An Essay on Keats's Treatment of the Heroic Rhythm and Blank Verse*. Paris, Hachette, 1909.

WORDSWORTH, WILLIAM: *Poems in Two Volumes* (1807), edited with "A Note on the Wordsworthian Sonnet," by Thomas Hutchinson. London, David Nutt, 1897.

INDEX

In the index all titles have been italicized, while first lines of poems have been indicated by quotation marks. Titles of poems by writers other than Keats have been followed by the author's name in parentheses.